Praise for *A Curriculum of Hope*

From the opening garden analogy onwards, *A Curriculum of Hope* is a delightfully written and intellectually rigorous attempt to do something that is so badly needed in current educational discourse. This is to consciously challenge unhelpful binary polarisation and find the much-needed middle-ground narrative that embraces the 'messiness' of learning and the innovative and creative practice that flows from it. *A Curriculum of Hope* is both a great addition to the debate and an excellent read!

Professor Samantha Twiselton, Director, Sheffield Institute of Education, and Vice President (external), The Chartered College of Teaching

The credibility of our national curriculum depends on the expertise of our teachers – in *A Curriculum of Hope*, Debra Kidd provides much-needed professional guidance. She motivates educators to seek empowerment and articulates a coherent strategy for teachers and school leaders to bring the curriculum to life in their classrooms and schools.

Ross Morrison McGill @TeacherToolkit – the UK's most followed educator on social media, who writes at TeacherToolkit.co.uk

Reading *A Curriculum of Hope* is like having a conversation with a fellow teacher. It features stories of real events in real classrooms, references to broader thinking and research, and humbling examples of what can be done to open up learning opportunities for our pupils.

This is a good book, full of concern for the best interests of all children. It explains how to help them learn and how we should decide what they should learn. That's what the most professional of teachers do. Debra is one of those teachers and a superb writer.

Mick Waters, Professor of Education, University of Wolverhampton

I love Debra Kidd's writing. She takes on the orthodoxies of the current educational establishment with wit, wisdom and a shining belief in the myriad, rich possibilities of education and our children.

Melissa Benn, writer and author of *Life Lessons: The Case for a National Education Service*

In this brilliant book, Debra Kidd manages to set out a curriculum concept rooted in reality, experience, joy and compassion. The structures, ideas and possibilities she shares will be invaluable to teachers, curriculum planners and leaders who desire to provide children with rich learning experiences that will have a powerful impact on their lives.

A Curriculum of Hope is an important book written by someone with a wealth of experience across the spectrum of education. It should be read, respected and acted upon. What a treat!

Hywel Roberts, teacher, author and storyteller

A Curriculum of Hope provides a considerable contribution to the debate surrounding curriculum. With razor sharp clarity, Debra Kidd identifies a number of problems with some wide-ranging 'umbrella' topics in the primary phase and proposes a clear rationale for developing content and concepts thoughtfully through threads. Debra makes the case that we need to ensure knowledge is utilised in ways that make learning effective for more than simply passing tests. She also provides some excellent examples for thinking about coherence across subjects in secondary schools.

Beautifully crafted and packed with insights, *A Curriculum of Hope* adds another dimension to the discussion about what it means to create a connected, compelling curriculum.

Mary Myatt, author of *High Challenge, Low Threat* and
The Curriculum: Gallimaufry to Coherence

A Curriculum of Hope

As Rich in Humanity as in Knowledge

Debra Kidd

Illustrated by Gabriel Kidd

independent thinking press

First published by

Independent Thinking Press, Crown Buildings, Bancyfelin, Carmarthen, Wales, SA33 5ND, UK

and

Independent Thinking Press, PO Box 2223, Williston, VT 05495, USA

www.independentthinkingpress.com

Independent Thinking Press is an imprint of Crown House Publishing Ltd.

First published 2020.

Independent Thinking Press has no responsibility for the persistence or accuracy of URLs for
external or third-party websites referred to in this publication, and does not guarantee that any
content on such websites is, or will remain, accurate or appropriate.

British Library of Cataloguing-in-Publication Data

A catalogue entry for this book is available from the British Library.

Print ISBN: 978-178135342-4
Mobi ISBN: 978-178135347-9
ePub ISBN: 978-178135348-6
ePDF ISBN: 978-178135349-3

LCCN 2019953042

Printed in the UK by
TJ International, Padstow, Cornwall

To the Pedagogical Activists of the World

Charlie McChrystal's council house garden was a bit of a mess. The inside of the house was spotless – my grandma made sure that every corner was cleaned within an inch of its life; the doorstep was whitewashed; none of their meagre possessions out of place. But the garden was overgrown with dandelions and buttercups.

Charlie McChrystal fought in the First World War. His first wife and their only child died in the Second. He was a broken, flawed man by the time I knew him, most alive and happy when distracted by Laurel and Hardy. As a child I was a little afraid of him, but every now and then a playfulness would break out in him and the sun would appear. It was rare, but we basked in the warmth of that sunlight when it shone.

Charlie McChrystal didn't talk about the war much. His sister told us how he had signed up with his friends from the small town they came from – Padiham in Lancashire – and how, when marching to the trenches of Ypres, he had stopped to pee behind a tree. As he looked on his pals were killed by a shell as they walked ahead. He never spoke of this to us, but even as children we knew he carried pain.

Charlie McChrystal wouldn't dig up dandelions. He wouldn't let others dig them up either. Because to him the dandelion was the only glimmer of hope in the hell hole of the trenches. The one 'bugger', as he put it, that you knew would survive. To his mind there were no weeds, just life.

Charlie McChrystal didn't value education much. He encouraged his own children to leave school and earn a living as fast as possible. They lived in abject poverty, and education was seen as a luxury they couldn't afford. When a neighbour donated a piano to the family, he chopped it up for firewood. But he fathered a child who would go on to encourage her own children to learn, whose mantra was 'Don't be like me – get an education.' Charlie McChrystal bred a rebel in Florence McChrystal. My mum. A dandelion.

I pray that we, and our children and their children, never see what Charlie McChrystal saw and that our world moves towards a time when no child or adult experiences the horrors of war or the kind of grinding poverty that my own parents grew up in. But if I say to teachers that we need to be the dandelions in the education system – pushing up through the cracks and resisting the performance-related pressures that can lead us to act without integrity or compassion – I hope that you will understand what I mean. And that you will take a moment to think of Charlie McChrystal, whose education and understanding of the world was forged in war and loss, but who nevertheless held on to hope.

Acknowledgements

This book would not have been possible without the brave teachers and heads I've encountered who have let me experiment with their curriculum models to test this work over decades. In particular, to Matthew Milburn and Helen Jones who, many years ago, entrusted their Key Stage 3 curriculum to me and set me off on this journey – thank you. To primary dynamo heads Andy Moor, Tina Farr, Julie Rees, Jenny Bowers, Richard Kieran, Vicky Carr, Sara Radley and Becky Bridges who have built humanity-rich curriculum models rooted in their local contexts but looking out across the horizon and beyond – you have been inspirational, and thank you for letting me play in your schools. To Sarah Smith in Pembrokeshire who allowed me and Hywel Roberts to plait the new Curriculum for Wales across the secondary school, asking big questions as we went along, and to Andrea Skelly who worked with us to build a humane curriculum in an alternative provision setting, thank you. To Rachael Mweti in Singapore who let me loose on the primary years programme, and Chris Waugh for generously sharing his work in New Zealand – thank you, too.

To my fellow curriculum explorer, 'sherpas' as he would have us known, Hywel Roberts – thank you for the collaborations, the friendship and the endless laughter. To the late Dorothy Heathcote who taught me how to guide children over the bridge of concern into genuine investment, and to Professor Mick Waters whose humour and wisdom have greatly influenced how I think and act and who is the most knowledgeable person I have ever met – thank you. To all those teachers who stand in front of children every day and who resist the mundane, the box-ticking and the pressure, and who change lives for the better – thank you.

Thank you also to Emma Tuck – the world's most thorough copy-editor and font of knowledge – this book is in much better shape because of you.

And to Gabriel Kidd and Beth Andrew for their artwork and plaits – a proper pair of dandelions – thank you.

Contents

'Hope' is the thing with feathers –
That perches in the soul –
And sings the tune without the words –
And never stops – at all –

Emily Dickinson

Introduction:
The Groundwork

Schooling is living, it is not a preparation for living. And living is a constant messing with problems that seem to resist solution.

Martin Haberman, The Pedagogy of Poverty versus Good Teaching (1991)

If schools were gardens, which one would you choose?

1. Everything is meticulously plotted out in rows. Every plant must have a utilitarian purpose, producing crops on the same day every year. Most of the garden must be given over to the five plants that the government have deemed most useful. The 30% of seedlings that are the slowest to grow are deliberately weeded out to create the impression of rigour in the system, in spite of the fact that they may have eventually thrived. Distraction from, or interference with, the main aim of producing crops is eliminated through the use of netting over the plants which keeps pollinators and birds at bay.

2. The garden has been left entirely alone in the hope that it will blossom into a wildlife meadow, attracting bees and butterflies. In reality, it is a mass of brambles, bindweed and knotweed, and the gardener dare not enter without protective clothing.

These are the two options that some factions in education like to suggest are available to us, with a fear of the latter driving many towards the former. Who wouldn't choose order over chaos and productivity over waste if they were the only options available? But they are not. Pretending they are is simply a tool of control designed to encourage people to adopt an 'official' model. Most sensible leaders and teachers know better.

There is a third option: we can have a garden that has multiple functions. It is a garden of remembrance but carefully planted to support the future. Some weeds are encouraged to grow because they bloom early in the spring and provide vital nectar for bees and other pollinators (hello, dandelions!). Among the statues, plaques and memorial benches are plants that feed us, plants that sustain other life forms, plants that simply make us happy with their beauty, colour and scent, and which remind us of the importance of such things in our lives. There are plants that heal us and plants that are rich in myths and stories. Our garden is a communal space, so there are places to sit, places to shelter, places from which to admire the wildlife and artwork we have attracted or placed there. We share it, grow within it and nurture it, and when we are struggling we call in others to help us to maintain and protect it.

Most sensible people will, of course, choose the third option. Most schools will claim to be the third, regardless of reality. But to have a truly integrated garden we have to be completely committed to the idea that education is about much more than produce; that difficult problems don't have easy solutions and that some easy solutions have unintended consequences; that sometimes you need to leave spaces for beauty and pleasure which all can share; and that we really need good, expert gardeners to keep the whole thing going.

Most of all we need to recognise that gardens are always in the present, no matter how much hope we are investing in the future. That rose won't bloom if there is not a constant daily process of feeding, deadheading, pruning and checking for predatory pests. The hostas will be shredded by slugs if we don't consider carefully where we plant them and how we protect them. To that end, we can spread poison in our garden or encourage hedgehogs, birds and toads to share our space. Every present choice has a future consequence – Haberman's messy living – and grappling with choices and consequences throughout the curriculum should be a child's entitlement, if we want them to understand how life works.

Maintaining hope is essential to gardening, but equally important is intention, planning and maintenance. This is a book about curriculum, so forgive me for labouring the metaphorical link to a garden. We might think of curriculum design as a form of garden design, but the design is inseparable from the act of gardening (the teaching and care of children) and from the forces that threaten our successes (the predators and pests we have to protect our garden from and that erode our sense of hope).

Some might argue that these pests come in the form of tests and accountability structures, but they're just weather. The real pests feed on our plants – the black spots of a lack of imagination, the fungus of apathy, the slug-like unquestioning compliance which leads to what Haberman describes as a 'pedagogy of poverty', where children have little opportunity to make choices or thrive in the here and now. A curriculum of hope is about much more than tests. It's about building a hopeful future in a productive present. Let's go back in time for a moment …

It was 2005. We had a new cohort of Year 7s in school and were writing a new curriculum. The results were pretty static and had been for some time, crawling along the floor targets. The students were compliant, most of the time, but largely apathetic. Everyone was working hard, but despite all that effort the school seemed to be coasting along. What could we do? At that time I was working partly in primary and partly in this secondary school. One of the reasons we were looking so hard at Year 7 was to ensure that the transition from primary to secondary didn't put limitations on young people and instead aimed to give them a chance to show us who they were and what they were capable of beyond what their data might suggest.

We had started off thinking about identity – a settling unit that allowed them to think about who they were, where they came from and who they might become, and to infuse that with some understanding of the place where they lived – at both a local and national level. We came up with the idea of an inductive unit of work where the students could design a 'Northern British Museum' in our school, bringing their knowledge across subjects to life by curating spaces for an exhibition for the local community. They would need to create exhibits to show what they knew and were beginning to understand about British history, geography, sport, literature, culture, science and so on, and to bring in some elements of their own experiences and those of their families in order to add a local dimension.

In effect, this transition period would be a means of mining their prior knowledge and building from where they were at. While some of their choices were predictable and might be seen in any school undertaking this task, anywhere in the country, some were more surprising. It became clear pretty early on that we were going to have a coal room. We were in Barnsley, and while the mines had gone, they cast long shadows over the lives of these young people.

Exhibited with love and care in the mining section of the museum was a lump of coal that one boy's granddad had carried out of the local pit on the day it was closed. There were also handwritten notes from Arthur Scargill, carefully folded newspapers which had been kept for decades, letters, diary entries, spoken word testimonies and more. Local families' lives and histories were given the same reverence as the exhibits celebrating Shakespeare and royalty. Seemingly disparate pieces of knowledge were lent a sense of purpose and coherence through the processes involved in deciding what was worth keeping and what had to be left out. It was the students, working in partnership with staff, who were deciding what the 'best which has been thought and said'[1] might be, and while the usual suspects were present, they brought these and other touching surprises to the table.

Shortly before we were due to open to parents, I found myself preparing some finishing touches with a Year 7 class: 'What we're missing is a statement piece. All great museums have one in their foyer: something – usually a statue – that gives us a sense of what the museum is about and what we might expect from it. Something about its values, maybe. If we had a statue that was a statement piece in our museum, what might it look like? What might the inscription carved into the stone plinth say? Can you create that for me, working in groups, as a still image? And write your inscription down on paper.'

They were off … We had carefully crafted our rules and expectations for effective group work over a number of weeks. Even the students who had come from primary with warnings practically tattooed on their foreheads were engrossed. Two of them held each other in an embrace – they had arrived labelled with 'anger management issues', accused of being unable to work cooperatively. Two Barnsley lads, clasping each other in an embrace, with no one around them batting an eyelid.

'This is ours, Miss – it's called Tolerance.'

....

1 M. Arnold, *Culture and Anarchy*, in *Culture and Anarchy and Other Writings*, ed. Stefan Collini (Cambridge: Cambridge University Press, 1993 [1875]), p. 190.

I was so pleased I took a photo – evidence, you see – but then I was distracted from behind.

'Miss! Can our statue move?'

I turned around.

'Statues don't usually move.'

'This one is mechanical and if you put 10p in it, it moves.'

I sighed and dug 10p out of my pocket.

The boys made their mechanical image. It began with a cricket match – one boy bowling, another batting. There were two fielders, hands held open in anticipation of a catch. I knew that England had won the Ashes that summer and this wasn't the first group of students who had wanted to have that achievement recognised in the museum. But when I put the 10p coin down, the tableau changed. The bowler moved one hand down towards the other – finger outstretched as if to press a button. The batsman and fielders turned their backs and crouched as if to protect themselves. And it was clear in that simple shift that we were now looking at the detonation of a bomb. For in the same summer the 7/7 bombings had taken place in London. I was silent for a moment. There was a lot to process.

'Do you want to know our inscription, Miss?' asked this 11-year-old.

'Yes please!'

'From Ashes to Ashes.'

I've redesigned many curriculum models in the last 15 years, but this moment shaped a lot of the work I have done because it reminded me of two important things when thinking about working with children: (1) give them the space to let them show you who they are and what they know, and (2) give them the space to let them show you what they worry about. And then attend to those elements. Too often as teachers we focus on the content to be delivered and too little on the recipient. Teaching is about being attentive to the conditions and the needs of those recipients. Yes, it's hard, but there's no point planting a sun-loving plant in the shade, and vice versa.

It has always seemed somewhat obvious to me that knowledge sits at the heart of learning. These children could not curate rooms about literature, history, sport, science, music, theatre or even coal mining without knowledge. But there was more going on here. There was an element of community – placing our work within the community, representing the community, inviting in the community. There was an element of creativity – not in terms of making, but in connecting our thinking and generating broader understanding. And there was compassion – not only in the way the children were acting towards others in their classes and beyond, but also compassion in the way that the curriculum acted towards them, in giving them space to build trust, to feel safe, to explore their hopes, dreams and fears, and in giving them the opportunity to have a voice.

It started me off on what has become a long journey of thinking about how curriculum acts as a vehicle for building what it is children need to know, but also a tool with which they can better shape their school experience, their relationships with others and the future world they will inhabit. I call this a humanity-rich curriculum, and at its heart are five pillars of practice which – in a humanity-rich, hopeful curriculum – will be plaited together as a set of entitlements for children. Just as a plant needs water, light, nutrients and protection from threats to survive, so a strong curriculum that supports the growth of children should have these five elements built in.

1. **Coherence:** The curriculum is planned and plaited so that it connects in sensible and logical ways, allowing children to build an understanding of ideas, concepts, chronology and themes, and to better understand them because they are encountered in a way that makes those connections explicit and relevant. (For more on curriculum coherence see Mary Myatt.[2]) Within a single subject, that might mean attending to the progression of ideas or to a chronology. Across subjects it might be that you consider mapping where there are touchpoints – which is easier to do in primary than secondary, but even here there are too many missed opportunities. For example, are the English department studying war poetry at the same time that the history

....

2   M. Myatt, *The Curriculum: Gallimaufry to Coherence* (Woodbridge: John Catt Educational, 2018).

department are studying the First World War? Are the geography and science departments coordinating their units on climate change? How does the context offered above for Key Stage 3 demonstrate how a shared purpose can create points of coherence for the students?

2. **Credibility:** The curriculum is clear about what children will know (propositional knowledge) and be able to do (procedural knowledge) and how these elements link to a prescribed national or regional curriculum, so that it is explicit how external expectations are mapped onto the internally experienced or enacted curriculum. Where a national curriculum is vague – for example, 'events beyond living memory that are significant nationally or globally' in the English national curriculum[3] – what knowledge are we choosing to teach and what do we want children to understand and be able to do with that knowledge? Are we making this explicit?

3. **Creativity:** The curriculum offers the child the right to experience, develop and practise creativity as an entitlement. Its view of creativity extends beyond making and doing in an artistic sense, and also allows for the development of fluency of knowledge and ideas through a process of interpretation, experimentation, connection and play. In the museum example on pages 3–5, the process of curation allowed the students to think about how to creatively link their knowledge, how to present it in an aesthetically pleasing and informative way, how to communicate the knowledge in order to capture the interest of the visitors and how to use a process of selection and rejection to organise and shape their knowledge – all aspects of the creative process.

4. **Compassion:** The curriculum uses a range of experiences, including stories, to allow children to develop empathy with other points of view and perspectives, and to use that empathy to move into active compassion. Active compassion is solution-focused and its aim is to move children beyond empathy towards action. As such, the compassion is symbiotic for the child: the child is encouraged to be a compassionate individual, but rather than being placed in a passive and potentially harmful space of powerlessness, is

---

3 Department for Education, *History Programmes of Study: Key Stages 1 and 2. National Curriculum in England* (September 2013). DFE-00173-2013, p. 2. Available at: https://assets.publishing.service.gov.uk/government/uploads/system/uploads/attachment_data/file/239035/PRIMARY_national_curriculum_-_History.pdf.

encouraged, through activities and outcomes, to be a powerful agent of change. The curriculum also acts compassionately towards the child in acting in his or her best interests – giving the child access to a full curriculum and activities that are known to impact on the mental health of the child – for example, physical activities and the arts.

5. **Community:** The curriculum is built with the broader community beyond the school in mind. Whether that takes the form of inviting in community members, building charitable and civic links of assistance, utilising the expertise within the parent body and local community, involving children in local democratic processes or arranging trips within the local area, community becomes a critical part of the curriculum design itself and not simply an appendage. Community is seen as a vital component of the cultural capital available to the school, so the school works in partnership with local organisations, theatres, museums and galleries to broaden the children's experience. A curriculum really rooted in community does not simply take advantage of what the community has to offer; it allows children to be of service to that community, shaping its future.

When these five pillars are in place, we see curriculum models emerging in which empowerment is the goal. Empowerment through knowledge, through action, through thought, through language, through play and, critically, through hope. This empowerment moves way beyond 'what works' in order to better pass tests, and moves towards 'what works' in terms of attending to the mental and emotional needs of children and to the present and future needs of the world around them.

This doesn't demand a great deal of extra work for teachers and schools, but it does ask that we refocus and consider the value of what we teach, the relationship of the content to other important ideas and experiences, and how knowledge, skills, emotion, action and experience can be plaited into lines of inquiry for children. These lines of inquiry come in the shape of questions that bind curriculum together and encourage a shared exploration of knowledge within rich contexts, forming 'grand narratives' of learning. Throughout this book I will share examples of how this plaiting is being developed in many schools, both in the UK and abroad, and explore how we can ensure that humanity and hope are not lost in our quest for results.

That is not to say that tests don't matter – at least at the end point of secondary education. They do for as long as they act as passes to the future. But in a great education, test results are by-products, not end products, and should never be the *raison d'être* for curriculum planning – a point made by Amanda Spielman in her commentary on England's new(est) inspection framework:

> A good curriculum should lead to good results. However, good examination results in and of themselves don't always mean that the pupil received rich and full knowledge from the curriculum. In the worst cases, teaching to the test, rather than teaching the full curriculum, leaves a pupil with a hollowed out and flimsy understanding.[4]

In England we are seeing a renewed interest in curriculum as a direct result of a focus on it in the new Ofsted framework,[5] and in Wales a new national curriculum due to be implemented in 2020 is forcing schools to look anew at how curriculum is structured and administered (for more on this see Chapter 6).[6] But the fact is that all schools, wherever they are and whichever curriculum overview they adhere to, need to look at how curriculum is enacted by staff and experienced by children. All models offer spaces for interpretation and innovation, and the best schools will modify and develop curriculum to suit the unique needs of their children and communities. It's not enough, or advisable, to buy a shiny, new (and undoubtedly expensive) off-the-shelf model. It needs to be crafted by the school stakeholders with love and care, and it needs to attend to the vital elements of power, ownership, responsibility, hope and humanity.

In this book, I will outline the key ideas underpinning this approach to curriculum design and explain why I think they are important. We will explore the role of pedagogy as a means of empowering children because, in my view, a curriculum of hope is delivered by a pedagogy of power. We will also explore some of the more overlooked pedagogical tools that we know can have great impact on children's learning and well-being – story, movement and play – as well as some of the

4 Ofsted and A. Spielman, HMCI's Commentary: Recent Primary and Secondary Curriculum Research (11 October 2017). Available at: https://www.gov.uk/government/speeches/hmcis-commentary-october-2017.

5 Ofsted, *The Education Inspection Framework* (May 2019). Ref: 190015. Available at: https://www.gov.uk/government/publications/education-inspection-framework.

6 See https://gov.wales/curriculum-wales-2022.

recent research into memory and retention. Towards the end of the book, from Chapter 6 onwards, there are case studies from some of my work in England, Wales and international schools, and an example of the system in New Zealand which has allowed some schools to plan in ways that allow for pupil choice, autonomy and responsibility – thanks to Chris Waugh for this section. There are some accompanying planning documents for these examples which you may find useful in the appendix (The Seed Catalogue). These documents are also available to download from the Crown House Publishing website.[7] A curriculum of hope depends on a generosity of spirit, and I thank all the teachers and leaders who have agreed to share our work in this book.

Scattered throughout, like dandelion seeds on the breeze, are tales of learning from the classroom, where this kind of curriculum planning and pedagogical approach is brought to life. They are examples of how children respond to this way of working – because none of this work has taken place in a theoretical space. It is the lived experience born out of real practice in real classrooms with real children over decades of teaching, and hopefully they will offer you some ideas about how this work might be constructed.

I haven't spoken much about early years education and curriculum, in part because I feel I have too little experience to make any meaningful contribution and also because there are enough non-early years specialists meddling in this area already with too little understanding of the developmental needs of very young children. There are, however, sections in Chapter 2 with regard to play that are pertinent and some examples of how some of this work might sit in a foundation class setting in Chapter 8. What I would say, however, is that no curriculum should ever have as its aim the spectacularly unambitious goal of simply getting children 'ready' for the next phase, which in many cases does not take into account the variances in development or indeed ages of children within a single year group. A good curriculum builds up, not down; it lifts children up, moving forwards and always working with the best interests of the children at heart.

While many systems are beginning to talk about a 'knowledge-rich' curriculum, we need to take care that knowledge is utilised in ways that make learning effective for more than simply passing tests. First and foremost, the knowledge should be important in its own right – in the here and now of the learning – so that children

----

7   See www.crownhouse.co.uk/featured/curriculum-hope.

can see the purpose of the knowledge in the context of rich dilemma and deep thinking. This book moves beyond knowledge and beyond the notion of the child as recipient, whose only mode of action lies in repetitive practice. That model – knowledge as compliance – is no better than any other. What we need instead is knowledge as power: power not promised in some distant vision of a university lecture hall or pay packet, but right here, right now in a child's lived experience. Knowledge as power in a curriculum of hope.

In a previous book I wrote the line 'for what are we if not architects of hope?'[8] In this book, I outline an approach for bringing that hopeful curriculum to life and offer examples from across the world of how schools are doing just that – despite the constraints of national, political and parental expectations. I have previously described this process as pedagogical activism – the small acts of resistance that teachers can implement in their classrooms to effect change. No curriculum can come to life without pedagogy. Curriculum may be the map, but pedagogy is the means of transport – and we have more autonomy than we think. It's time to flex our muscles. Like weeds growing through cracks in concrete, hopeful and humane curriculum models are flourishing, and this book celebrates them.

Walk with me. We walk in hope.

---

8   See H. Roberts and D. Kidd, *Uncharted Territories: Adventures in Learning* (Carmarthen: Independent Thinking Press, 2018), p. 1.

Chapter 1

Getting Weedy

The Art of Resistance

A core curriculum?

Let's say …

A new minister for education is appointed in a new government in a new political party, the likes of which we have never seen before. Swept in on a tide of hope, they stand poised to make their mark.

This human being looks at the vast task ahead of them. It's daunting but they're proud. They don't know much about education; they weren't state educated themselves and it's a long time since they were at school, but they want to do a good job. They want to make their mark. It's only human.

How does one make one's mark in politics? There are two ways: to act wisely and carefully with long-term goals in mind or to act expediently with short-term goals in mind. Our current political system very much favours the latter approach, and so our well-meaning, well-intentioned but ultimately inexperienced secretary of state makes their first mistake – putting the survival and progression of career and party first.

Short-term goals attract media attention – the message must be sharp and enticing. Our minister examines the zeitgeist. They make a proclamation: the education system is 'broken' but they intend to 'fix it'. A few skewed statistics playing on deep parental fears is all it takes. Attention is paid and reform is promised.

The fix must be quick. Ideally it won't involve changing the law, which takes time, so the curriculum is obviously the place to start. And so we come to our second strand of human fallibility. The minister, suspicious of 'experts' who may not be politically aligned with them, decides to make their own decisions. It is decided that the solution is perfectly simple: 'Look at me – I'm successful. What led me here was my education (in the fervour of the moment they forget about their economic advantages, sociocultural privileges and connections). What I had, all children should have. What I learned, all children should learn. What I am passionate about, all children should be passionate about!'

The minister sits at a desk, pondering what may be missing from the curriculum. And there in the fruit bowl is an apple. A light bulb goes on.

'What could symbolise this nation more than an apple?' they think, leaping from their seat with excitement. No matter that the apple comes from Central Asia – the minister is fondly remembering long summers in the country, the orchard, the sound of bees and the clinking of tea cups in the garden. In their mind, the apple becomes synonymous with all that will make this nation 'great again'.

And so, one Saturday morning, as the weekly education briefing email lands in the inboxes of head teachers across the nation, it is declared that apples are to form a cornerstone of the new 'heritage and health' curriculum. And, by Monday, apples are being discussed in every staffroom in the land.

The minister is pleased but uneasy. These teachers are a tricky bunch. A lot is resting on the success of this project. The eyes of the world, and the boss, are on this new idea. It has to work. And so within a month, a small team of graduates (with no teaching experience) have whipped up a policy document listing the minimum expectations around the teaching of apples and neatly listed them into objectives:

- Pupils should learn to identify at least three types of apple.

- Pupils should know that apples grow in temperate climates.

- Pupils should be able to identify an apple as a fruit and name other fruits.

And so on …

Just to make sure, the minister adds a test – an apple 'check' – and declares that the results will be published, that all children will take the check at the same time, regardless of their age, and all must be above average. The media laud the rigour and glory of the new curriculum. Teachers and mathematicians sigh.

The curriculum lands in my inbox along with an email asking me to lead on the teaching of apples. At that point, as a teacher, I have a choice. I can take each one of those dry objectives and allocate a lesson to them. I can begin each lesson with the objective written on the board and get the children to dutifully copy it down, providing evidence for when OrchEd come knocking on the door. I can weave in lots of retrieval practice in preparation for the check. I can create dual-coded resources to aid memorisation. I can even try to liven things up a bit by putting bowls of chopped apple out on tables for the children to taste so they can complete the table on their worksheet. And when all the children – dry and dull but compliant and capable – pass the check, I can put up a banner outside the school.

Or, I can ask myself, 'What is interesting about an apple?'

I might think about incorporating the apple into a much bigger unit of work on Fibonacci, the golden ratio and symmetry in nature, because I've identified a need to get children excited about maths.

I might consider whether it's true that 'an apple a day keeps the doctor away' and incorporate my teaching of apples into a much wider unit on human health, looking at the impact of antioxidants on the body and exploring whether some apples are better than others in this respect.

I might go further and ask more philosophical questions about the apple. How has it come to be a symbol of knowledge? Why was it traditionally given to teachers as a gift? Why is it that in Western depictions of the story of the Garden of Eden it is an apple that Eve plucks from the Tree of Knowledge, yet in Islamic depictions of the story it is a pomegranate?

I might reflect on how our climate and geography, our flora and fauna, impact on our social, cultural and religious icons. How do these shape our stories, our myths, our legends? Can it explain why an apple is sometimes regarded as dangerous (Snow White, Alan Turing)?

I might look at the mythology around the logo of Apple Inc. and why it is so richly steeped in all of the above …

Within all of these possibilities, I could take care to weave in the relatively low-level knowledge that our new minister requires. I would take care to ensure that my children passed the test – oops, sorry, the 'check'. But they would be bright-eyed, curious and much more knowledgeable as a result of these latter choices. Under this interpretation, there is no need for banners outside of school because the children run home to talk about their learning. Their parents spread the word. And before long, people are knocking on the doors of the school asking to come into the Garden of Eden.

....

When schools start to think in these ways – finding the core, if you like, the potential areas of interest in a curriculum – many things change. It is not simply that the knowledge is somehow richer or more powerful. There is a deep impact on the attitudes of children towards learning and their perceptions of self. In the words of one parent of a child in a primary school with whom I have been working:

> My daughter spent the first three years at school feeling 'stupid' (her word) and being told she was never going to reach her target. With the new curriculum she comes home quoting facts and information, wanting to discuss topics in a way she has never done before. She's far more engaged and has completely thrown us with her depth of knowledge and understanding of topics/issues. The curriculum has allowed her to progress and grow in a way she couldn't before. She is not afraid and will try anything given to her.

Words like these, let loose into a local community, do far more for the reputation of a school than any inspection report (although what kind of inspector wouldn't value this too?). What would parents say about the way curriculum is delivered to children in your school? About how their children see themselves as a direct result of their experiences and interactions in school?

The limitations of a 'national' curriculum

It seems fitting that the word curriculum has its roots in the Latin *currere* – to run a course. It seems that is what we do: set children off on a race, with the expectation that there will be winners and losers. A running course has no diversions or tributaries. Taking a break is frowned upon. And, what's worse, in our current system there are no staggered starts. We turn a blind eye to the fact that some children will need to run further and harder than others in order to try to end up at the same point. In his book *Thinking Allowed*, Mick Waters refers to the searing inequalities of the 'inside lane' and 'outside lane' (or 'gutter') in this race and our inability to adequately provide structures to support those on the outside.[1] In the recently published Timpson Review into exclusions in England and Wales, we see a worrying trend towards bumping children off the track in the pursuit of appearing to have improved the outcomes of a school.[2] Weeding them out of the system altogether.

Our notion of what a curriculum is has been increasingly lost to the desire to show improvement through testing. Waters is careful to point out that a curriculum should always be more than a national curriculum which only sets out minimum expected standards of study. For many schools in England there is no need to even adhere to the standards of the national curriculum since academies and free schools are exempt, while in other countries the curriculum is sufficiently vague as to allow for a great deal of interpretation through the 'enacted' curriculum. This means that teachers have more freedom than we like to think we have when deciding on how the curriculum we enact in our schools will impact on children.

In designing your own curriculum model, you are shifting towards creating your 'school curriculum', which Waters simply outlines as:

The school curriculum comprises the elements that young people need:
- to nurture them as individuals and meet the hopes we have for them
- and help them to appreciate their community
- so that they learn about their county, country, the world and the universe
- and it includes the national curriculum.[3]

1 M. Waters, *Thinking Allowed: On Schooling* (Carmarthen: Independent Thinking Press, 2013), pp. 21–37.
2 Department for Education, *Timpson Review of School Exclusions* (May 2019). Command Paper 92. Available at: https://assets.publishing.service.gov.uk/government/uploads/system/uploads/attachment_data/file/807862/Timpson_review.pdf.
3 Waters, *Thinking Allowed*, p. 267.

What kind of curriculum holds hope for young people and for the world they will inhabit and shape? What kind of curriculum helps children to appreciate their community (rather than encouraging them to get the hell out of their community)? What kind of curriculum looks beyond the national, the immediate, the tyranny of the test and builds this kind of learning experience? Perhaps it is one that resists the notion of learning as a race and instead embraces it as an exploration. What if, instead of running to the end point of the education system, or even to the end of a unit of work, the purpose of the course lay in the journey itself? What might that course look like?

By using the example of the apple, I am trying to make the point that we always have choices. As teachers, whenever we set off on a curriculum journey, we have the power to decide whether the children need to get from A to B directly and expediently via the quickest mode of transport; whether to take the scenic bus route and take in the sights along the way but end up efficiently and predictably at the end point; or whether we walk in a spirit of adventure, happy with some diversions but with a map in our hands. I think most teachers would agree that it is probably best not to get lost altogether – the model which might be better known as chaos but which some mistakenly confuse with 'discovery' or 'inquiry'.

It will all be dependent on what you are learning and why, and there are opportunities and pitfalls with each approach. The skill lies in choosing the most appropriate method to suit your purpose. I would argue that the teaching of phonics is probably deserving of the Central Line, but many other areas of learning can be plaited into a good walk with a map. It is this aspect of curriculum – that which sits outside of the mechanics of phonics, number bonds or times tables – that is the focus of this book. It concerns the teaching that is situated in the realm of understanding who we are, where we come from, what we might become and how we impact on those around us. The big questions of education and of life.

When it comes to curriculum design, and to many areas of educational discourse, what we are seeing right now is a battle between models of thought around systems, structures and people. We can conceptualise these as gardens or journeys or apples, but they are fundamentally situated in a conflict around ideas. I suspect that we would all be better off if we considered that some ideas suit some purposes and others suit other purposes – a horses for courses approach. But that becomes difficult because too much of education and other areas of social policy are really about power and control and being seen to be 'right'. It's exhausting. All a teacher can really do is to make sure that they keep children's experiences as broad and rich as possible. It's not a question of teaching like no one is watching. There are always around 30 people watching – they are the ones to whom you need to attend.

The philosopher Gilles Deleuze's description of an architectonic model[4] closely mirrors much of what we are currently seeing being advocated as a well-designed, knowledge-rich curriculum model – something tightly sequenced and controlled, with the content decided by a higher authority and then reliably 'delivered' to the passive recipients. Under the architectonic model there is a hierarchical relationship between the mind of the designer and the matter it works upon – in this case, the child. It is therefore necessary to view the designer as the 'expert' and the child as the 'novice'.

Standing in-between is a worker – someone who carries out the architect's tasks in order to realise his or her vision. Their duty is to pass on this vision as accurately as possible – uninterpreted and unsullied. We see this in some schools in the form of scripted lessons which are written by managers and delivered by technician teachers, often unqualified or in training. The idea is that the lesson, designed by an expert, can be reliably passed through a conduit because the content is reliable and the reaction of the recipient is predictable.

A belief in such a system is entirely dependent on the notion that it is possible to know how material will be received, understood and processed. It is interesting that this curriculum vision has grown in line with a trend in education to seek pedagogical certainty from educational research. The possibility that other factors might influence the design through-line is disruptive to the ideology, and therefore all distractions and outliers must be eliminated. Draw the blinds down if it snows! Remove dissenters from the classroom! Provide not only a script but a cross on the floor for the teacher to stand on to ensure they don't deviate from the plan! It's a garden of artificial, plastic plants.

It's not clear where the motivation for all this comes from – probably a range of sources. For some organisations it's an attractive business proposition: sell an off-the-shelf curriculum model with assurances that 'it will work'. For others it might

---

4 See D. Kidd, *Becoming Mobius: The Complex Matter of Education* (Carmarthen: Independent Thinking Press, 2015).

seem like a seductive way to reduce workload and effort around planning. For some fiscally squeezed senior leaders the prospect of being able to ensure 'quality', by having scripted resources delivered by cheap and unqualified staff, must be tempting. But it's an illusion. Children are not predictable and neither are the communities in which they live.

No matter how many blinds we pull down, all curriculum is received by a complex adaptive system in the form of the brain of a child, and in such systems no one intervention can ever function without impacting on, and being impacted by, other unforeseen elements. Any architectonic model relies on the recipients being predictable, and on the perception of those who don't respond in the expected way are deviant or at least inconvenient to the functioning of the system.

As I wrote in *Becoming Mobius*, in many systems of education there is a hierarchical imposition of will. Some of this is a matter of necessity. Schools are publicly funded and accountable as a result of this funding, so there needs to be some element of hierarchical order for the system to function. But it seems that many nations have gone too far in this pursuit of control (while paradoxically promoting it as 'freedom of choice'), and we are reaping spoiled crops as a result. A rise in mental health problems among young people is one area of concern, as is the pernicious influence of fake news and an unwillingness to engage with complexity. It seems to me that we are getting things very wrong, and in the process we are in danger of removing hope from children at the very same time that we are claiming to champion their needs.

Nowhere is this more obvious than in the authoritarian reactions to climate change protesters around the world who have been inspired by Greta Thunberg. Here we have children taking an active part in the democratic processes they have been taught about in school. They are utilising their knowledge – exhibited in banners and placards that refer to temperature, sea levels, CO_2 emissions and more. They are using their literacy skills to articulate their concerns. They are navigating transport systems to travel and connect. They are taking what they have learned in history to impact on the future. As one young protester's banner said, 'Missing History; Making History!' Twelve-year-old Sam, writing in his school's newsletter, communicates the seeming hypocrisy of learning something in school then being punished for demonstrating that knowledge: 'What is the point of learning about people who broke the rules, like Nelson Mandela or Rosa Parks, when we are not allowed to break the rules ourselves, even to save our own species from extinction?'

What these children are doing is taking what a curriculum could be and enacting it in front of educators. They are utilising the knowledge acquired in classrooms and beyond, blending it with their technological understanding of social media (learned how?) and combining it with a deep sense of ethical justice. We should be following them down the streets and gathering this wonderful evidence of learning for our files and inspections. Instead, we get this from England's Secretary of State for Education Gavin Williamson: 'They should be learning, they shouldn't be bunking off and it's very irresponsible for people to encourage children to do so.'[5]

Knee-jerk reactions such as these automatically pit children against the adult world and highlight the tensions that arise when you educate young people but expect them to do nothing with their education until they have left school. It is no wonder then that some of them are resisting. From the March for Our Lives teens in the United States, to the growing international band of climate activists, to Malala and her campaign to educate girls across the globe, we are seeing the rising phenomenon of children taking matters into their own hands. Some regard these children as weeds to be removed and controlled. Others see them as beacons of hope. What they are doing (like buttercups and strawberries) is creating rhizomatic networks that elude and subvert the systems under which they have been raised. Whether they are products of, or resistance against, their education systems is anyone's guess. What is clear is that they are determined to shape their own world.

In his book *Forget School*, Martin Illingworth documents how this trend is impacting on the world of work as record numbers of young people either choose to, or are being forced to, work for themselves, thereby avoiding traditional career routes and job security.[6] He discusses the shift towards freelance working within a gig economy, which – for better or worse – is how young people are increasingly likely to be earning their living. If we accept that a large proportion of our school population will be responsible for their own tax and pension affairs, what are the implications for the curriculum in our schools?

5 BBC News, Climate Strike: Thousands Protest Across UK (20 September 2019). Available at: https://www.bbc.co.uk/news/uk-49767327.
6 M. Illingworth, *Forget School: Why Young People Are Succeeding on Their Own Terms and What Schools Can Do to Avoid Being Left Behind* (Carmarthen: Independent Thinking Press, 2020).

While I recognise the 'education for education's sake' argument, we nevertheless, surely, have a responsibility to be equipping young people with the tools they will need to navigate this world. Passivity or a lack of agency could be a catastrophic hindrance to this generation. I would argue that in the same way that they need to read, they also need to practise the skills and attributes that a life of independence and self-reliance will demand of them. This is not a matter of 'jobs that haven't been invented yet' (although who would have seen blogger, influencer, YouTuber or gamer coming along 20 years ago?); this is more of a 'jobs that used to be secure but no longer are' reality. To maintain hope in this world, children need the tools necessary to develop acumen, resourcefulness and a capacity to not just cope with but utilise uncertainty.

In addition to adapting to shifting patterns of work – even without going into the impact of artificial intelligence which we know is likely to bring 'profound change to the world of work'[7] – we can already see a significant and influential minority of young people who are pioneering new ways of thinking, interacting, protesting and being. They are rejecting traditional ways of doing things, bypassing what they see as the apathetic and inactive systems of adulthood, and forming their own alternatives and possibilities.

What can we do to make schools into places where this idealism and energy can be harnessed and encouraged? My view is that this doesn't lie in talk of the future; it lies in the present lived experience of the classroom. A classroom in which the teacher doesn't have to talk about the future because the present comprises of all the conditions, forges all the habits of mind and introduces all the knowledge from which the future, whatever form it takes, can be navigated.

Much of this kind of learning is deeply emotional, so we need to attend to the idea that emotions can drive learning in positive and constructive ways (for more on this see the pedagogic tools explored in the next chapter). We know from psychological research that human beings are both goal-orientated and emotional and that these can both enhance and impair learning.[8] In a nutshell, curiosity and interest tend to have positive effects and boredom and anxiety negative impacts.

....

7   British Academy and The Royal Society, *The Impact of Artificial Intelligence on Work: An Evidence Synthesis on Implications for Individuals, Communities, and Societies* (2018), p. 19. Available at: https://www. thebritishacademy.ac.uk/sites/default/files/AI-and-work-evidence-synthesis.pdf.

8   See M. Smith, *The Emotional Learner: Understanding Emotions, Learners and Achievement* (Abingdon and New York: Routledge, 2017).

Working in positively emotional and hopeful ways requires that classrooms provide the conditions from which rich lives can emerge but also meet the demands of our education system. It requires professionalism and imagination to find and develop the kinds of contexts for learning that make children feel invested in the here and now of their learning experience, while also attending to their possible future needs.

Too often we impose a fear of the future onto young people, adding threats of dire consequences or promises of glory to their future selves in order to make them comply in the present. But our goal should be thriving in the present. I was drawn to the beauty of this observation by Ben Newmark: 'Our curriculum should whisper to our children "you belong. You did not come from nowhere. You are one of us. All this came before you, and one day you too might add to it." '[9]

The curriculum should indeed make children feel that they belong, that knowledge is theirs for the taking, that they should be hopeful that they too can add to this rich human heritage. But it also needs to whisper to children that they matter now, that they can do something now, that they are not powerless or passive but that they are active agents of learning.

What does that kind of curriculum look like? A hopeful curriculum is one that uses hope and empowerment as a lens through which we might select what and how we teach. For example, if we have a primary national curriculum which states that we ought to teach the ancient Greeks, we are immediately faced with choices. For a start, it is simply not possible to teach around 3,000 years of history, mythology, political and sociological processes and all the attendant belief systems, geography and events in a six-week block of afternoons interrupted by other aspects of subject and curriculum. If we're not careful it becomes a patchy mess of tasks and disconnected facts with a dressing-up day thrown in for entertainment. We have to choose.

In a more traditional setting, the unit may be broken up into a knowledge organiser with key facts set out alongside a timeline. The children will be expected to know the names of a few principal players – perhaps gods or Pericles. They may

---

9   B. Newmark, Why Teach?, *BENNEWMARK* (10 February 2019) [blog]. Available at: https://bennewmark.wordpress.com/2019/02/10/why-teach.

be tested on this knowledge, but whatever is chosen, more will be left out than finds its way in. This is inevitable in every model.

In a hopeful, humanity-rich curriculum there will be a different lens. The curriculum will operate on two time levels; the 'then' time and the 'now' time, so the children are actively experiencing the history while also developing skills that are relevant to their current and future lives. For example, they may be placed in the position of being advisers to King Acrisius of Argos who has learned from the Oracle at Delphi that his grandchild will grow up to kill him. The story might act as a vehicle to learn some facts: where is Argos? What were city states? What was the Oracle? What were the belief systems of the ancient Greeks? Where did the story of Perseus come from? How was Mycenae founded and by whom? What is the timeline of the empires of ancient Greece?

But they are learning just as much about living today: how to talk to powerful but dangerous people or how to persuade someone against taking an unethical course of action. By asking the children to design a prison for Princess Danae that permits her some comfort, the teacher is gently encouraging the children to think about finding hope in dark places. The possibilities are endless, but they are not accidental and must be planned for alongside the knowledge. The compassion and creativity are as important as the credibility of knowing.

In a hopeful curriculum, the 'there' place is connected to the 'here' place, just as the 'then' time is connected to the 'now' time. The dilemma of an ancient mythological king is connected to their own dilemmas in communicating with others. The ancient place is connected to their own experiences of power and fear and agency in their lives. The big questions draw the two together: are human beings in control of their lives? What is fate? How do you speak truth to power? These are golden threads of connected meaning.

To do this effectively we need to place children knee-deep in dilemma – to let problems and difficulties drive learning – and yet do all of this in a playful, joyful and hopeful space. Of course there are people who will say that children should be seen and not heard. That they should smile and not complain. That they should obey and not question. That they should be grateful for the crumbs of knowledge given to them. They are probably not reading this book. You are. So let's think about how we might proceed, and why.

Chapter 2
Tooling Up
The Pedagogy of Power

In my last school, we developed a 'triple A' pedagogy built around autonomy, articulacy and activity.[1] The founder of School 21 in London, Peter Hyman, sets out a similar vision in which the child is encouraged to engage head, heart and hand in learning to make full use of the intellectual, emotional and physical processes that can help them to learn and, indeed, live.[2] As the advances in cognitive science and neuroscience develop more and more ways of being able to explore learning in young people, we are seeing increasing evidence that learning is both a multisensory and an emotional process, and that there are some important and powerful tools we can engage to embed understanding.

We know from the work of neuroscientists such as Antonio Damasio and Andrew Curran that learning is deeply emotional and that our reasoning is streamed through and infused with emotion.[3] In his book *The Emotional Learner*, Marc Smith outlines three main domains of learning – the emotional, the social and the cognitive – and argues that these are closely intertwined. He warns against the oversimplification of regarding learning as merely a shift in long-term memory: 'The process of learning certainly requires the engagement of cognitive processes, but without other so-called non cognitive processes, learning simply will not take

1 D. Kidd, Bouncing on a Bed of Knowledge (Or It's All About the Pedagogy, Stupid), *Love Learning* (8 May 2013) [blog]. Available at: https://debra-kidd.com/2013/05/08/bouncing-on-a-bed-of-knowledge-or-its-all-about-the-pedagogy-stupid.

2 P. Hyman, A Curriculum of Head, Heart and Hand, in R. Blatchford (ed.), *The Secondary Curriculum Leader's Handbook* (Woodbridge: John Catt Educational, 2019), pp. 13–27.

3 A. Damasio, *Descartes' Error: Emotion, Reason and the Human Brain* (New York: Random House, 2006); N. Humphrey, A. Curran, E. Morris, P. Farrell and K. Woods, Emotional Intelligence and Education: A Critical Review, *Educational Psychology* 27(2) (2007): 235–254. Available at: https://www.researchgate.net/publication/233473746_Emotional_Intelligence_and_Education_A_critical_review.

place. The process of learning, therefore, involves cognitive, emotional as well as social processes.'[4]

These emotional processes, along with research concerning physical processes such as embodied and grounded cognition, go way beyond some of the more utilitarian work around simply retaining information for tests, although that is not to say those can't be useful. However, if we want a curriculum model that allows children to experience and practise the complexity of life, we need something much more powerful than retrieval practice.

What we are starting to understand when it comes to learning is how complex the process is, and yet that there seem to be certain things that work for most people. If we want to get children to remember information, for example, we know that regular, low-stakes testing/quizzing helps,[5] and that it's better if that testing is spaced or looped so we keep going back to pick up on threads, like a backstitch. We also know that interleaving information – interrupting it with unrelated information but then coming back to the original focus of study – seems to be effective.[6] I would argue that it is more effective, however, when it is interleaved with material that is in some way conceptually or thematically connected.

We tend to be very unimaginative in terms of thinking how these techniques might work outside of a formal drill-and-test structure. Situating children within stories in which they work through dilemma can be an extremely effective way of interleaving information. We can use the narrative to interrupt and reinforce the learning, as well as deploy questions both in and out of role to practise retrieval. Similarly, some project-based learning approaches allow for effective interleaving because children switch their attention between the different demands of the project. These approaches are not incompatible, and the time wasted in tribal positioning has been very damaging to the profession as a whole. As Mick Waters says: 'The ongoing debate … has skewed understanding and distorted consideration of children's wider needs. It leads to petty squabbles and point scoring, jockeying for position and territorial behaviours. The bigger picture gets lost.'[7]

....

4 Smith, *The Emotional Learner*, p. 7.
5 H. L. Roediger III, A. L. Putnam and M. A. Smith, Ten Benefits of Testing and Their Applications to Educational Practice, *Reading Research Quarterly* 21(1) (2011): 49–58.
6 P. C. Brown, H. L. Roediger III and M. A. McDaniel, *Make It Stick: The Science of Successful Learning* (Cambridge, MA: Harvard University Press, 2014).
7 Waters, *Thinking Allowed*, p. 272.

If we want a broad and balanced curriculum, the bigger picture needs to be held in mind, and with it a broader, possibility-focused vision of what pedagogy can be.

The power of story

The ancients understood the power of story to unite communities, build identity and make sense of the world. From creation stories to myths and legends, religious texts and parables, stories have long been the vehicle through which human experience is interpreted. Perhaps it's no surprise then that stories are considered by cognitive scientists such as Daniel Willingham to be 'psychologically privileged' in the human mind.[8] Borrowing heavily from E. M. Forster's *Aspects of the Novel*, Willingham breaks down the elements of story that the human brain connects with into the four C's – causality, complication, conflict and character. When these four elements are in place, children are far more likely to recall information than they are when that information is presented in expository form.

This work has prompted many to think that if they simply read stories that contain curriculum knowledge to children, the job is done. But things are more complex than that. For a start, Forster is at pains to explain a key difference between story and plot – or events and causality. He offers this example:

A plot is also a narrative of events, the emphasis falling on causality. 'The king died and then the queen died' is a story. 'The king died, and then the queen died of grief' is a plot. The time-sequence is preserved, but the sense of causality overshadows it … Consider the death of the queen. If it is in a story we say: 'And then?' If it is in a plot we ask: 'Why?'[9]

What a teacher can add to this plot is a pivot of action. A pivot would shift the story from being passively to actively received: 'The king died, and then the queen died of grief, and now her children need our help.' Or 'The king died and then

---

8   D. T. Willingham, Ask the Cognitive Scientist: The Privileged Status of Story, *American Educator* (summer 2004). Available at: http://www.aft.org/periodical/american-educator/summer-2004/ ask-cognitive-scientist.

9   E. M. Forster, *Aspects of the Novel* (London: Penguin, 2005 [1927]), p. 87.

the queen died of grief. How might their lives be remembered and commemorated?' Placing the children within the story with a job to do is one way of bringing the cognitive, emotional and social aspects of learning together – a little like bringing light, water and nutrients to a plant.

A critical element of the memorability of narrative rests on this notion of causality – the 'why' of how things happen. But there is more. How many of us have read and enjoyed books but subsequently been unable to recount the plot – the trace of our memory is often simply the feeling the book has left us with. It would seem that narrative is a good starting point for remembering (partly, perhaps, because it engages our emotions and appeals to the brain's pattern-making tendencies in setting out chronology and order), but in order to make the learning truly memorable we need to layer in additional connections.

Adding a pivot to the story brings in the children directly. It forces attention and possibility so that they are responsible for the story. Getting children actively engaged in the narrative means adopting roles and responsibilities, and we are beginning to learn a little about why this is such a powerful pedagogic tool. Cognitive science has called it the 'Batman effect'.[10] While the initial research was with very young children, it goes a long way to explaining the reported effects from teachers who work with role on how learners exhibit heightened language skills, concentration and perseverance when working in this way.

This goes beyond simply enacting a role; it also links deeply to the brain's ability to develop and 'practise' states of being. According to Christopher Bergland, 'Because our brain's neural circuitry is malleable and can be rewired through neuroplasticity, one's tendency for empathy and compassion is never fixed. We all need to practice putting ourselves in someone else's shoes to reinforce the neural networks that allow us to "love thy neighbor as thyself".'[11] One possible way that teachers can utilise the Batman effect to develop not only perseverance but also compassion is to place the children into role and deep dilemma.

....

10 R. E. White, E. O. Prager, C. Schaefer, E. Kross, A. L. Duckworth and S. M. Carlson, The 'Batman Effect': Improving Perseverance in Young Children, *Child Development* 88(5) (2017): 1563–1571.

11 C. Bergland, The Neuroscience of Empathy, *Psychology Today* (10 October 2013). Available at: https://www.psychologytoday.com/gb/blog/the-athletes-way/201310/the-neuroscience-empathy.

Kieran Egan's work on narrative breaks the process down even further.[12] He places stories within the framework of what he calls our 'cognitive tools', which he categorises as somatic tools (our embodied cognition, emotions and senses), mythic tools (our language and communication tools which we utilise in order to make sense of the world), romantic tools (driven by a desire for transcendence from reality – the realm of the imagination), philosophical understanding (making connections to build grand narratives and abstract thinking) and ironic understanding (our ability to read between the lines and surmise subtext and layers of meaning). Egan argues that stories are uniquely placed to utilise all of these tools, and that we pay too little attention to their power when we design curriculum or plan our lessons.

At the most basic level, these tools engage body, emotion, intellect and imagination and create a powerful web in which we can trap learning and memory. And to properly utilise the body, emotion and mind – to do, feel and think – children have to be *in* the story for it to have the most impact.

Of course, there are elements of the curriculum and areas of human endeavour and achievement that are more utilitarian, and it may not be necessary to evoke stories in order to teach them. But it would seem that recently, certainly in the West, our focus has been almost entirely on this realm of utility in which we are encouraged to believe that the only way to really learn stuff is to repeat, practise, test and practise again. That's all well and good, and can be useful to teachers, but it's an overly simplistic model and one that doesn't serve children well if we want to prepare them for a complex world.

On the other hand, a desire to occupy children through empty but entertaining task-setting is no better. There is little value in making Stonehenge out of biscuits, for example, simply in order to find something 'fun' for the children to do. These kinds of tasks are distractions. What we need to find is a means by which children experience and engage with what Christine Counsell describes as 'an indirect manifestation of knowledge'.[13] She also discusses the 'hinterland' of learning – the

---

12 K. Egan, *The Future of Education: Reimagining Our Schools from the Ground Up* (New Haven, CT: Yale University Press, 2008), pp. 33–86.

13 C. Counsell, Senior Curriculum Leadership 1: The Indirect Manifestation of Knowledge: (A) Curriculum As Narrative, *The Dignity of the Thing* (7 April 2018) [blog]. Available at: https://thedignityofthethingblog.wordpress.com/2018/04/07/senior-curriculum-leadership-1-the-indirect-manifestation-of-knowledge-a-curriculum-as-narrative.

place where story is powerfully connected to the knowledge: enhancing, connecting and utilising it rather than distracting from it. Counsell offers some strong examples of how this hinterland might be used in class, but it is still offered as something external to the children – by definition, distant to them. I would argue that a far more powerful means of engaging children in powerful knowledge is to place them right in it: a 'hitherland'.

In order to place children *in* a story, rather than situate them simply as recipients of a story, the learning is necessarily active and verbal. Vocabulary and action sit at the heart of this work, so the teacher is very engaged not just as a deliverer or facilitator but as a multifaceted and adaptive force for change. In this realm of story, the teacher can be she who knows. Or who doesn't know. Or who litters the classroom with the debris of difficulty, throwing obstacles in the way in the form of questions. Whatever role the teacher plays, they are always deeply present, agile and skilled.

I'm teaching Year 3 in Singapore. We've created a mountain community by drawing zigzag lines across A4 pieces of paper and putting them together to make a mountain range (thank you, Hywel Roberts, for this idea). From the shapes of their drawings we've deduced whether this is (geologically speaking) a new or an old mountain range and how we might be able to tell. I've thrown in my own drawing too – one of my mountains has a flat top and some smoke coming out of it. There is a village at the bottom of this particular mountain and the children have populated the area with other geological and geographical features – glaciers, rivers, waterfalls, lakes, caves, forests, craters and crevices. We stand back and look at our work.

Child A: There's an active volcano near that village!

Teacher: How do we know it's active?

Child A: It has smoke coming out of it. We'll need to keep an eye on that.

Teacher: Why would anyone want to live near an active volcano?

Child B: It makes the soil fertile. Lots of active volcanoes have people living close to them – the ash and lava put nutrients in the soil.

There are a few moments of silence while we take this in. I didn't know that a child in the class knew this stuff – I'd been planning to teach it in the form of a grumpy farmer who is annoyed with scientists trampling his field. But they already know. I go into role as the grumpy farmer, nevertheless, and I point out that this volcano has smoked on and off for almost 200 years but not erupted. He dismisses the children's concerns.

We call an emergency meeting.

Teacher: Let's say that the volcano has started spewing ash into the air and that the alert level has been raised to 3 or amber. What if it was our job to evacuate the village? What might we need to think about?

The children quickly list things we would need to do and assign tasks – within minutes they have a team of volcanologists, a medical team, a police unit to keep order and an evacuation team who have to look at transport options. They even have a team of vets and animal rescuers, a team who are in charge of evacuating the school and a group who have to design and resource an emergency shelter.

I place a square of masking tape on the floor representing the boundary of the village, with one line heading out to the south and another north to the mountain. I write on the northern line 'Farm 1km'. I'm weaving in some practice of mapping skills and compass points, but there is no need for me to write them as objectives on a board.

Teacher: What's the difference between a city and a village? What might we have in a village?

We renegotiate the likelihood of finding large shopping malls and condos in a village and settle instead on a grocery store, a farm shop and small houses. The children start to ask some questions.

Child C: There's only one road out of here! Is there a train station?

Teacher: No, and no airport either. You didn't put one in, so we only have the road.

Child C: We could use helicopters and land them in the field.

Teacher: Can helicopters fly through volcanic ash clouds?

Child C: I'll go and find out.

Child D: We can use the river too – we can take boats downstream.

Teacher: How far do we need to take people before they're safe?

Child D: I don't know.

Teacher: Find out – how fast does pyroclastic flow travel, and how far does it go?

Child D runs away to find out.

Child E (tugging at the teacher's sleeve): We are the medics – we need masks. Volcanic ash solidifies in the lungs. We need to give people face masks to help them to breathe while we move them.

Teacher: How many do we have?

Child D: 120

Teacher: But there are 500 people.

There's a long and thoughtful silence.

Child D: We could ask ladies to use their bras as face masks. We could cut them in two.

No amount of planning can prepare you for that. But being aware of the need for questions that push children further, building spaces for thinking time, demonstrating with poker-faced conviction that the child is perfectly capable of solving the problems you're throwing their way – all these things create the conditions under which the child will often surprise. Giving a little information but not quite enough, pressing upon them the urgency of a situation but within the safe space of playfulness, and constantly but carefully folding facts into the story so that they shine with the polish of being immediately useful and relevant to the situation we're in, these all make the learning deeply memorable. We're not mucking about here. This is serious play.

In the process of their preparations, and by giving regular briefings and submitting written responses, the children find out:

- What causes a volcano to erupt.
- What has happened during volcanic eruptions in the past.
- The impact and effects of volcanic ash and lava.
- Emergency protocols.
- The role of infrastructure in disaster management.
- The speed at which ash, debris and lava can travel.

- Modes of transport and their relative speeds.

- The differences between rural and urban developments and between agricultural communities and industrial communities.

- How to persuade people to leave everything they have behind.

- Materials that may be resistant to volcanoes (e.g. titanium – sadly we didn't have time to construct a titanium barrier!).

And:

- Alternative uses for women's underwear.

They have also engaged on a higher level with some conundrums: who do we prioritise in our evacuation and why? Do people have the right to choose to stay and risk their lives? Who will be the last to leave? Why do people choose to live in dangerous places? Are some people more likely to live in dangerous places than others? And so on.

Ultimately, however, the children have been empowered to enact solutions. They haven't simply sat and learned about a natural event that will in all likelihood never impact directly on them (although living so close to Indonesia it might). It doesn't matter because the story *has* impacted directly on them – they were there, at the edge of a volcano, and they had choices to make. They won't forget.

Of course, there are moments in processes such as this when we gather information. When I teach, explicitly, elements of vocabulary and information they might need. In these instances the children are eager to learn from someone who knows because they have a need to know too. I throw obstacles in their way, creating desirable difficulties – 'that's too slow/too expensive/too risky' – to make them reach further, think harder, overcome problems. Because that is what they will need to practise in life. The volcano is just the beginning.

When planning these ways of working, Hywel Roberts and I encourage teachers to start with the story that will ignite the thirst for more knowledge – knowledge that has to be (a) acquired and (b) utilised in order to learn. We place this story in a frame because stories or plots are dramas, and dramas always involve a human being in a mess.

People
Who is the human being in a mess? Who else might have alternative perspectives in the story?

Place
Where and when does this take place? How does the setting and time create opportunities for learning?

Problem
What is the mess? Where are the tensions, complications and difficulties?

Possibilities
What are the solutions? How do those solutions drive possibilities for curriculum coverage?

The power of play

When we live in a society obsessed with getting ready for the next stage of life, we tend to push pressure downwards in an age group. Nowhere has this become more obvious than in England, where baseline testing for 4-year-olds is being trialled under the banner of 'school readiness'. Coupled with reports written by the government's school inspection regime, Ofsted, such as *Bold Beginnings*, there is a clear shift towards formalising education for the youngest children in the school system.[14] Such a philosophy is alien to much of the rest of the world. Even in Singapore, formal schooling doesn't begin until the year a child turns 7 and most countries in Europe follow the same pattern. That is not to say that informal learning means no learning. In most developed countries early years education is serious business – it utilises the power of play to develop the social, linguistic and self-regulation skills that children will need in the future. It is on these foundations that more formal learning like reading, writing and numeracy are built. And for good reason.

A study by Stanford University in 2015 found that children who delayed school by one year demonstrated better levels of self-regulation at the age of 11, with fewer children diagnosed with attention deficit hyperactivity disorder.[15] We also know that self-regulation is a key indicator of future academic success,[16] so it would seem that developing this capacity in younger children impacts on their success in secondary education too. The compelling case for play-based informal education is summarised in a report by David Whitebread of the University of Cambridge, in

---

14 Ofsted, *Bold Beginnings: The Reception Curriculum in a Sample of Good and Outstanding Primary Schools* (November 2017). Ref: 170045. Available at: https://assets.publishing.service.gov.uk/government/ uploads/system/uploads/attachment_data/file/663560/28933_Ofsted_-_Early_Years_Curriculum_ Report_-_Accessible.pdf.

15 T. Dee and H. Sievertsen, The Gift of Time: School Starting Age and Mental Health. NBER Working Paper No. 21610 (2015). Available at: https://www.nber.org/papers/w21610.

16 A. Duckworth and S. M. Carlson, Self-Regulation and School Success, in B. W. Sokol, F. M. E. Grouzet, and U. Müller (eds), *Self-Regulation and Autonomy: Social and Developmental Dimensions of Human Conduct* (New York: Cambridge University Press, 2013), pp. 208–230. Available at: https://repository. upenn.edu/cgi/viewcontent.cgi?article=1002&context=psychology_papers.

which he points to a number of international studies that have shown considerable benefits from delaying formal education and immersing children in play.[17]

Whitebread argues that play has formed an important part of our evolutionary development – something we see in young mammals who practise their play-fighting, play-hunting and societal structures in safety under the watchful eye of adults until they are ready to enter the adult world. But humans use play for more functions than other mammals. They also create and imagine through play, and use this to innovate and adapt the environment and materials around them so that they don't have to wait for evolution to do this for them. This makes the connection between play, language, imagination and socialisation even more important for humans, and not just for young children. It forms the basis for both scientific and artistic thinking and experimentation. This is more than just the Batman effect – it also seems to be connected to well-being and development.

Children tend to focus their play in five key areas:

1. **Physical play:** development of body, coordination, gross and fine motor skills.

2. **Manipulations:** interacting with objects, experiencing scientific concepts such as weight, speed, density, texture and forces.

3. **Social play:** role playing and stories – the development of language and social interactions, empathy and perspectives.

4. **Symbolic play:** meaning making, developing understanding of abstract thinking and aesthetics.

5. **Games with rules:** developing concepts of fairness, order, social structure and safety.

There is no area of the more formal curriculum that doesn't utilise at least one of these skill sets, so introducing children to the formality before this play stage has been explored is an interruption to, not an acceleration of, development.

In their report on the neuroscience of play, Claire Lui and colleagues outline five principles of playful experiences that are helpful for teachers when thinking about

17 D. Whitebread, M. Basilio, M. Kuvalja and M. Verma, *The Importance of Play: A Report on the Value of Children's Play with a Series of Policy Recommendations* (Brussels: Toy Industries of Europe, 2012). Available at: http://www.importanceofplay.eu/IMG/pdf/dr_david_whitebread_-_the_importance_of_play.pdf.

the kinds of opportunities they open up for children and which enhance development.[18] The principles are:

1. **Joyful:** Developing a positive experience of learning through play increases levels of dopamine in the brain, which at the right levels can enhance not only learning and memory but a general feeling of well-being.

2. **Meaningful:** Making meaningful connections between novel stimuli, materials and situations not only stimulates creativity, but also memorable learning, problem-solving and positive attitudes to change and difference.

3. **Active engagement:** Both physical and intellectual engagement with tasks develops concentration, coordination and is linked to feelings of reward and satisfaction.

4. **Iterative:** Placing deliberate difficulty into the play so that children have to persevere and solve problems builds resilience, neural pathways to make connections and a sense of purpose and reward.

5. **Social interaction:** Playing with others develops not just language skills but also emotional regulation, empathy, fires up mirror neurons to build the capacity to understand others' perspectives and develops a sense of social order, norms and values.

When reading the above list, it's hard to argue for a case that play should stop at a certain age or that it is only necessary in early childhood. In the description of multi-modal inputs and the powerful ways that these inputs impact on development and learning, we see echoes of other theories of learning, such as dual coding, emotional learning and embodied cognition. This multi-modal way of learning seems to allow children to process all kinds of stimuli without overloading working memory. In addition, playing with ideas, stimuli, situations, objects and others is healthy and helpful for all human beings, whatever their age. Indeed, recent studies have argued the case for adults to be more playful, citing advantages in mental health, creativity and social bonding.[19] For these reasons – far more compelling than the much maligned 'fun' – a curriculum of hope places playfulness

....

18 C. Lui, S. L. Solis, H. Jensen, E. Hopkins, D. Neale, J. Zosh, K. Hirsh-Pasek and D. Whitebread, *Neuroscience and Learning Through Play: A Review of the Evidence* (Billund: LEGO Foundation, 2017). Available at: https://www.legofoundation.com/media/1064/neuroscience-review_web.pdf.
19 See C. D. Magnuson and L. A. Barnett, The Playful Advantage: How Playfulness Enhances Coping with Stress, *Leisure Sciences* 35(2) (2013): 129–144.

alongside stories as a key pedagogical cornerstone to create a knowledge-rich and humanity-rich curriculum.

The power of movement

Cognitive science is producing some interesting and important work around memory, and this field is evolving quickly. Every time I write a book, new research has emerged by the time it is published. When cognitive load theory was first introduced as a means of explaining why we don't always remember what we are told, it was presented in such a way as to suggest that the best way to reduce overload was through explicit, teacher-led instruction in which distractions and interactions are limited to allow for concentration to be focused on content.[20] This then evolved, with an acknowledgement that complex tasks might best be done in groups to reduce the cognitive load on the individual,[21] and more recently to the relationship between mind and body in managing load and understanding concepts.[22] Research around embodied and grounded cognition suggests that learning is complexly situated in body and mind, and that it may well be that utilising the body can help children to remember more effectively.[23]

This is not to suggest that there is no place for simple, straightforward, explicit teaching; there is, and a good teacher will switch modes as necessary. A teacher might teach a concept or idea in science quite formally, but then move to a more active means of allowing the children to process and practise their new knowledge. For example, in the science classroom described by Carolina Kuepper-Tetzel, creating 'embedded phenomena' – physical re-enactments of scientific concepts – had

20 J. Sweller, Cognitive Load During Problem Solving: Effects on Learning, *Cognitive Science* 12(2) (1988): 257–285.

21 P. A. Kirschner, J. Sweller, F. Kirschner and J. Zambrano, From Cognitive Load Theory to Collaborative Cognitive Load Theory, *International Journal of Computer-Supported Collaborative Learning* 13(2) (2018): 213–233. Available at: https://doi.org/10.1007/s11412-018-9277-y.

22 F. Paas and J. Sweller, An Evolutionary Upgrade of Cognitive Load Theory: Using the Human Motor System and Collaboration to Support the Learning of Complex Cognitive Tasks, *Educational Psychology Review* 24(1) (2012): 27–45. Available at: https://link.springer.com/article/10.1007/s10648-011-9179-2.

23 A. Noë, *Out of Our Heads: Why You Are Not Your Brain, and Other Lessons from the Biology of Consciousness* (New York: Hill & Wang, 2009).

a significant impact on the performance of all children, but specifically on those who were considered to have low spatial reasoning ability (considered to be a key indicator of likely success in science learning).[24] It would seem that in addition to the emotional engagement of stories, the physical engagement of movement can act as a powerful tool for learning – and, of course, the two are connected through play.

Research in this area is still developing and there has not yet been enough time to fully gather data on a scale that would show replicable steps. However, there seems to me to be some logic in applying the Counsell 'hinterland' principle to movement as well as narrative. The test is whether the movement or physical representation activity is related to the knowledge being taught or extraneous to it.

Some years ago, I found myself teaching a GCSE history class to cover for a period of staff absence. The students were approaching their exams and feeling anxious. They had been taught an acronym by their teacher to help them remember the causes of the First World War: MAIN (militarism, alliances, imperialism, nation-alism). Although they could remember the letters, they were struggling to remember the actual words that were, in theory, supposed to unlock the relevant information. I had been reading some emerging research into muscle memory at the time and suggested that they add a movement to each word that represented its meaning. We had a series of suggestions: making a 'gun' with the hand for mil-itarism, hugging yourself for alliances, puffing out the chest and jutting out the jaw for imperialism, and waving a flag for nationalism were just some of the sugges-tions. The students chose the ones they felt resonated best for them. We then went on to encode the key elements of each cause, first in labelled diagrams (I had not heard of dual coding at that point but it seemed instinctively to make sense) and then by attaching small movements. We applied the same process to other aspects of revision, creating a multisensory loop of movement, language and image.

It was back in the day when teachers were allowed to be in the exam room at the start of exams as a reassuring presence for the students. I stood at the front of the room and watched as they turned over the paper. There were three GCSE history groups dispersed throughout the room, but you could tell where these particular

----

24 C. Kuepper-Tetzel, Embedded Phenomena: Increasing Comprehension of STEM Concepts Using Body and Space, *The Learning Scientists* (21 September 2017) [blog]. Available at: http://www.learningscientists.org/blog/2017/9/21-1.

students were. They were twitching. Not the full movement range – that would have been horribly distracting for others – but small gestural twitches. A clasp of a fist, a slightly jutting jaw … I noticed them move and then write, move and write. One looked up at me and winked. Most of those students did rather well. I can't put it down solely to the few lessons I had with them, but I know that the movement, if nothing else, helped to trigger the knowledge that someone else had painstakingly taught them.

In this example we see how knowledge might be utilised to aid revision through what is called the 'enactment effect',[25] but being physical in the classroom has all kinds of other benefits,[26] not least in supplying the brain with oxygen and the obvious and well-documented mental health benefits. Perhaps more surprisingly, Lyelle Palmer's work in the United States has shown gains in reading and phonological knowledge when movement and play are incorporated into teaching.[27] There seems little doubt that activity offers a positive means of achieving learning outcomes in a way that is more interesting and beneficial to young people. We seem to be missing a trick, as Paul Howard-Jones puts it, in not utilising this more in our classrooms.[28] He points to recent research which shows that the enactment effect leaves a trace in the brain – what we might think of as a memory forming part of a schema – and argues that this is a potentially powerful but very underused process in most classrooms. It would seem that we are moving towards a greater understanding of how mind and body work together to aid learning, and how we might use this most effectively in the classroom.

Like anything else, however, it needs to be done with thought and care. In my experience, movement, like narrative, is most powerful when it is usefully combined

....

25 H. D. Zimmer and R. L. Cohen, Remembering Actions: A Specific Type of Memory?, in H. D. Zimmer, R. L. Cohen, M. J. Guynn, J. Engelkamp, R. Kormi-Nouri and M. A. Foley (eds), *Memory for Action: A Distinct Form of Episodic Memory* (New York: Oxford University Press, 2001), pp. 3–24.

26 A. Singh, L. Uijtdewilligen, J. W. R. Twisk, W. van Mechelen and M. J. M. Chinapaw, Physical Activity and Performance at School: A Systematic Review of the Literature Including a Methodological Quality Assessment, *Archives of Pediatrics and Adolescent Medicine* 166(1) (2012): 49–55. Available at: https://jamanetwork.com/journals/jamapediatrics/fullarticle/1107683.

27 L. L. Palmer and B. DeBoer, Enhancing Early Reading Recognition and Phonemic Awareness with Neuro-Educational Programming: The Minnesota SMART Project (Stimulating Maturity through Accelerated Readiness Training). An Interim Report (May 2014). Available at: https://actg.org/sites/actg.org/files/documents/MinnesotaSMARTProject_May2004.pdf.

28 P. Howard-Jones, *Evolution of the Learning Brain: Or How You Got to Be So Smart …* (Abingdon and New York: Routledge, 2018), p. 166.

with knowledge to aid conceptual understanding. We return to Hyman's words, where 'head, heart and hand' are powerfully engaged in learning and where we move both physically and metaphorically towards greater understanding in order to build a more hopeful future.

Utilising these three approaches in teaching demands something of the teacher and of the curriculum itself. There is a demand on time – building stories and exploring through movement and play isn't something that can be 'chunked up' into neat lessons with starters, mains and plenaries. Putting learning objectives on the board spoils the surprise somewhat. Even having books for writing which are separate to books for learning can undermine the process. We have to be dandelion-minded in our planning.

The story – the enticement into learning – gives the learners the early pollen they need to sustain their interest in the learning. The deep tap root allows them to draw from a well of knowledge and to survive when difficulty is thrown their way. And the light and seemingly fragile seeds generated by the inquiry and exploration disperse, settle and take root in other areas of the curriculum and in broader skills – enhanced vocabulary, purposeful writing and applying ideas to other topic areas. Planning documentation won't be based around individual lessons, but across the arc of a learning journey; around medium-term plans in which the five pillars are plaited into a unit and in which these plans feed into a longer term vision of learn-ing across the whole year and beyond. A curriculum of hope is designed to thrive and connect.

Chapter 3

Plaits and Umbrellas

Finding Coherence
Across the Curriculum

In recent years some people have become quite cross about cross-curricular learning. Even the attempt to rebrand it as 'interdisciplinary learning' has met with derision from some subject purists. This way of working has been derided as being superficial, lacking in rigour and a threat to the very identity of the teacher. Much of what has been said about cross-curricular or interdisciplinary learning stems from the belief that to work in this way is to water down learning rather than enhance it, and to undermine the subject knowledge of the professional teacher.

It is true that, without care, working in a cross-curricular way can lack in depth and purpose. But when done well, cross-curricular learning offers great potential for children to reach across subjects, connecting learning within and across domains of knowledge. It can strengthen schemas, act as a means of interleaving content and make for powerful and meaningful learning. As Mick Waters writes:

> Teachers who are true subject enthusiasts know that their subject discipline is a living thing to be enjoyed and explored as it unfolds in the modern world. The best educated, however, are not limited by subjects but possess that critical skill of making those vital connections between disciplines.[1]

In primary schools, cross-curricular learning has long been a tradition, labouring under the label of 'topic' or 'theme'. Sometimes this work is brilliantly woven together, but too often it becomes a hotchpotch experience in which subjects are tenuously crammed in to meet the demands of a national curriculum without any real coherence. Some of the topics learned beg the question of what is actually being learned (I'm looking at you, 'Superheroes'!). In my (probably unpopular)

1 Waters, *Thinking Allowed*, p. 288.

opinion, it is not enough to settle on a topic simply because it will be fun. School days are too short. At their best, topics should build broad cultural capital and vocabulary as well as knowledge. They should enhance children's understanding of who they are, where they come from and how they connect to the world through time, place and experience. They need to embed big questions about the world and get children, in the words of Hywel Roberts, 'bothered'.[2] That is not to say they can't be playful, powerful and active – they can – but they need to be meaningful too.

One of the reasons that topics like 'Superheroes' appear on school curricula is because of the belief that in order for learning to be relevant to children, it needs to link to their existing interests. This is a mistake. Relevance is not about limiting learning to the existing interests and experiences of children; it's about finding the universalities of human experience that allow children to find relevance in seemingly irrelevant or distant curriculum content – to find what binds and connects us. It's to make learning matter. You can do this for 'Superheroes': I taught a session with Year 1 in which their beautiful town had been wrecked by a local superhero, Lava Lady. It involved learning about volcanoes, urban design, fireproof materials, costings, negotiations and understanding that positive motivations can sometimes have negative impacts. But they could have learned all of those things if I had just taught volcanoes really well too (remember that Year 3 class on pages 30–34?).

We shouldn't shy away from more difficult or abstract content with children just because it seems irrelevant to their lives. Our job is to find the relevance, the fascination, the wonder and make it irresistible to learn. But this need not be done in tight subject-related straitjackets.

Nevertheless, the purpose and content of any topic or project needs to be clearly and carefully thought through. Mary Myatt writes about creating a 'curriculum map' and avoiding unclear and tenuous links. You can almost see the twinkle in her eye as she writes about this on the theme of water: 'In Religious Education this gets translated into Jesus walking on water. And yes, he probably would have wept.'[3]

What Mary describes here is what I call 'umbrella planning', in which a topic has been decided upon and all subjects are expected to form spokes to hold up the umbrella. Some spokes will be strong. Others not so much.

....

2 H. Roberts, *Oops! Helping Children Learn Accidentally* (Carmarthen: Independent Thinking Press, 2012).

3 Myatt, *The Curriculum*, p. 22.

'Water cycle!' yells geography excitedly.

'Swimming!' sighs PE.

'Jesus!' whispers RE.

Umbrella planning can work well when you have a great topic that lends itself to all subjects, but even then links that might have seemed obvious to staff during planning don't always make sense to the children. We still need to make these links explicit. We also need to be clear about where the different subjects will appear within an interdisciplinary unit of work, how different subjects have different ways of approaching the problem or issue, and how they might elicit different kinds of responses.

Coherence across the curriculum is easier if, instead of conceptualising planning as an umbrella, we think instead of a plait into which we weave the knowledge we need as we go along. This allows us to select content more carefully: do we need it now, later or not at all? It's about moving away from 'we could do' to 'this is what we need to do'. We could do all kinds of things in school, but when we plan like this we tend to run away with ourselves. Plaiting around a problem or a story keeps us on track.

For example, I have to teach the Romans to a Year 4 class. But I'm a visiting teacher and I don't know what the children already know, or what the teacher usually teaches, so I'm looking for a way in. Procrastinating as usual on Twitter, I come across an exchange in which classical scholar Mary Beard is gently trying to explain that there were indeed black soldiers in the Roman army and that the portrayal of them as such by the BBC was not in fact 'political correctness gone mad'.[4] As soon as I see mention that Syrian soldiers were posted on Hadrian's Wall, I'm off. The 'then' time and 'now' time colliding are enough. Within 24 hours I'm sitting in front of a class of Year 4 pupils, but they could easily have been Year 8.

I begin by miming an action – carving something – and I ask the children to watch. It's an idea I've taken from Tim Taylor's work,[5] and I'm careful when they question me afterwards to weave in the notion of being homesick.

4 See https://twitter.com/wmarybeard/status/889925415032299520?lang=en.
5 See https://www.mantleoftheexpert.com/resources/planning-units/context/the-roman-legionnaire.

Child A: What's your favourite colour?

Teacher: Blue because of the sky in my beloved homeland.

Child B: What's your favourite food?

Teacher: The pomegranate that grows on the tree in my father's garden.

In this way there are no 'low-level' questions – teacher agility means I can take each question and elevate it into something significant.

They question our Syrian auxiliary soldier, Theoteknos (a name I have chosen so that we can explore the idea that Syria was occupied by the Greeks before the Romans), and discover how far he has travelled and how he lives his life. They are learning all they 'need' to know about the life of a Roman soldier on Hadrian's Wall and more. Plaited into this is the concept of homesickness: the climate and flora of a distant land; the plight of refugees today; the power and powerlessness within an institution like an army. These are not tenuous links. They are tendons connecting time and place.

When they track his journey on maps and their little fingers drift across the Mediterranean Sea, they are tracing the journeys of all who have crossed her, in hope or in fear, then or now, and we can open up a wormhole of time travel – if we want to. Is the crossing of an ocean history or geography? Does it matter? Theoteknos' story is the vehicle through which we can learn about day-to-day life on Hadrian's Wall, the development of local towns and villages, and the interdependence of them and the garrison. We can learn about life in Roman Britain but also gain a broader view of the size and scale of the Empire, of the structure of power, of systems of governance. Looking at maps of Roman Britain and comparing the 'then' places to the 'now' places is a simple plaiting of two subjects – and we can easily add more.

In this primary school example, the Romans is the 'topic' and it's easy to see how it can be plaited. But in a secondary setting it might more easily be woven into a broader curriculum question around movement and migration, and neither approach would be lacking in coherence. In a secondary model, the students might look at this Roman story in English and history but also explore migrations of people linked to the movements of tectonic plates in geography.

They might investigate molecular movement in science or physical movement in PE, movements in music and drama, the story of migration in food and so on. None of these are in themselves without significance in their own right, but together they form vibrations – a curriculum in motion. There is no expectation that science teachers will talk about Romans. They don't have to bend tenuously to another subject's focus. But they and others are bound by an echoed language – a rhythm of the curriculum. Movement of people. Movement of things. Movement of time.

Or they might not. Other echoes might be found. The important thing is to look for them, find them and make them explicit to the learners. Subjects do not exist in isolation from the world (for more on this, take a look at the section on the Curriculum for Wales in Chapter 6).

One way of planning for coherence is through planning for progression – mapping out the way propositional and procedural knowledge will develop (see the planning example in The Seed Catalogue for geography). Some schools, like St Catherine's Catholic Primary School in Sheffield, have found SOLO taxonomy a useful tool in this respect.[6] For example, skills progression in history might involve pupils being able to 'interpret' a source – i.e. identifying what is happening to whom, done by whom, at a descriptive level; being able to 'analyse' the source – identifying facts and elements of bias; and then, as capability progresses, moving towards being able to 'generalise' – exploring the significance and impact of the source in relation to other sources and events. The school's deputy head, Jonathan Lear, says that conceptualising the progression of skills in this way has been helpful in mapping out a sense of coherence across a subject which is separate but connected to the acquisition of factual knowledge.[7]

One thing that most people seem to be agreed on is the idea that the brain forms schemas while learning, and these can be helpful in building new learning that may be connected in some way. But schemas don't fit into neat subject boxes. When learners are forming these blueprints of learning they will construct a series of

6   See http://www.johnbiggs.com.au/academic/solo-taxonomy/.
7   J. Lear, Conference Keynote. Speech delivered at the Bringing the Curriculum to Life conference, Blackburn, 29 November 2019.

synaptic connections which create a 'web' – parts of this web will be factual but much of it is sensory and emotional. If someone has learned 2 + 2 = 4 in a cold room, for example, they may associate the information with being cold. For me, 7 x 8 = 56 will always be accompanied by the sting of a ruler hitting my palm. Our senses attach themselves to our learning like sticky willy weed, so they need to be attended to. Building positive learning experiences involves taking into account the emotional state of the learner and the physical conditions of the environment. This can lead some to eradicate distraction (no displays, blinds down, track the teacher) or others to make learning deeply sensory and emotional. Stories, outdoor learning, tactile materials and play would all fit in the latter model. I would argue that as well as enhancing learning, they also lead to more positive attitudes to school.

One of the jobs of a teacher is to try to help the child to (a) construct new schemas and (b) strengthen these connections so that learning can be readily accessed and used to make new connections. We know that repetition can be helpful – repeated actions help to create a myelin sheath around synapses which allows information to be accessed more quickly – hence the emphasis on repetition and practice. But we also know that multisensory stimuli have a powerful effect and these can't always be accounted or planned for. If I smell eucalyptus I can tell you which tree it comes from, describe the tree and, from that, recount experiences of seeing eucalyptus in Australia – but I'll also be in my grandma's house in Melbourne, sipping a strawberry milkshake with my toes in a paddling pool. Memory is always complexly interwoven with other stimuli. We can ignore that 'other' or we can utilise it. We can draw down the blinds or we can make the day the elephant walked past our classroom window a joyful memory that connects to the learning we did. And we can strengthen schemas by plaiting connections between subjects and topics.

The big question, then, is: at which point does the story (or the multisensory learning) become extraneous load which distracts from, rather than enhances, the learning? To mitigate this potential problem we need to ask ourselves whether the task is relevant to the matter being learned or to the problem being solved. An important question to satisfy, in their recounts of what they have done, is whether the children are clear about what they have learned.

Plaited planning is skilled work. It starts with a context, and content is woven in as it is needed. It requires patience – you need to leave some gaps for the children to fill in and bring their own knowledge to the work. The questions they generate can help you to plan forward, weaving them in as you go. Most of my plaited planning requires revision almost as soon as a session has taken place. Sometimes it will be rewritten retrospectively, taking into account what has happened in a session. It takes knowledge and an understanding that you can't cover it all – it is better to go deep than wide and shallow. You may begin with a context – a Celtic king deciding whether or not to capitulate to Roman demands. Or a Syrian auxiliary soldier standing alone on Hadrian's Wall and feeling homesick. Or a fisherman sitting with his head in his hands on a boat in AD 79 watching Vesuvius erupt and destroy the city where he has lived all his life. But you still need to know why.

In this work, the story drives the knowledge – forming the hitherland of the curriculum – and becoming the place where problems become possibilities. Solving problems, as we know from Daniel Willingham, is deeply satisfying and memorable, flooding our reward systems with dopamine.[8] If we already know that stories are deeply memorable, then we have to conclude that solving a problem within the framework of a story has the potential to be very powerful indeed.

These plaits provide us with a way forward by bringing together what have been unhelpfully considered the binaries of progressive vs. traditional. For example, when Clare Sealy writes about 'links' in curriculum planning[9] and I speak of 'echoes', we are effectively thinking in similar ways about plaiting ideas together. She offers an example from her own school in which children encounter the concept of tyranny first in Year 1, learning about King John, and subsequently in Year 5, learning about Dionysius I of Syracuse in their study of the ancient Greeks. By the time they encounter Hitler in Year 6 the notion of a tyrant is well embedded. The word tyrant echoes down the curriculum line, perhaps reinforced by encounters with the etymology of *Tyrannosaurus rex* or by the appearance of tyrants, despots and dictators in other subjects and texts. The concept of tyranny echoes through the curriculum, plaited in and building not just knowledge but also vocabulary.

Sealy's article describes making links not just vertically (in terms of age progression) but also horizontally (linking subjects across a year) and diagonally (allowing

8   D. T. Willingham, Why Don't Students Like School? Because the Mind Is Not Designed for Thinking, *American Educator* (spring 2009). Available at: https://www.aft.org/sites/default/files/periodicals/WILLINGHAM%282%29.pdf.

9   C. Sealy, The 3D Curriculum That Promotes Remembering, *Primarytimerydotcom* (28 October 2017) [blog]. Available at: https://primarytimery.com/2017/10/28/the-3d-curriculum-that-promotes-remembering.

concepts to make connections across age and subject), forming the three strands of a plait at a whole-curriculum level.

For secondary schools this thinking can be particularly helpful:

1. **Vertical:** What will Year 7 learn that is separate to but conceptually and linguistically connected to what they will need in Year 11? (How do the key concepts and skills that bind our subjects connect to build deeper understanding? For example, in science, rather than teaching 'forces' as a unit of physics, could we plan to show how forces impact on our biology and our chemistry as well as on our physical world, revisiting the concept in many guises over time?)

2. **Horizontal:** What might connect our subjects across a year group so that learning is more connected conceptually? (What might a history curriculum look like that had 'power' as a connecting theme or concept across a year?)

3. **Diagonal:** Where are the touchpoints between our subjects and our year groups, so the students learn that there are conceptual and linguistic complexities and interpretations which might be viewed differently (and similarly) within and across our subjects? (For example, in English, could they encounter a text with a similar theme (man vs. nature, perhaps) in each year as they progress up the school? How might that theme connect with what they are learning in geography (natural disasters), science (climate change), history (the eruption of Mount Tambora and its impact on European history) and so on?)

Conceptualising planning as a plait has been helpful to me in my practice, finding ways to allow learning to flow and make better sense for children, and permitting them some sense of ownership in planning forward. I refer to plaits frequently in subsequent chapters as I explore in more detail some examples from secondary and primary settings both here and abroad.

Chapter 4

The Wasteland?

Curriculum in the English Secondary School

Let us be clear that the feat that every secondary school has to perform each year, getting 200 or so 16-year-old students to sit 25–30 exams in one month requires a level of organisation, regimentation, control and relentless drive that is so harmful, distorting and unnecessary that any hopes of a broad curriculum is nothing more than a dream.

Peter Hyman, 'A Curriculum of Head, Heart and Hand' (2019)

It is four years since Ofsted published its somewhat damning indictment of the English Key Stage 3 curriculum (age 11–14), stating that education for this age group was simply 'not a priority' for too many leaders in English secondary schools.[1] Since then, the new linear GCSE examinations have pushed more and more English secondary schools towards implementing a three-year GCSE programme, in spite of the courses being designed to run for two years, prompting the chief inspector of schools, Amanda Spielman, to warn against the narrowing of the curriculum offer in these vital middle years of education.[2]

Indeed, a survey of teachers by the National Foundation for Educational Research found that in a small but significant number of schools, GCSE preparation was

1 Ofsted, *Key Stage 3: The Wasted Years?* (September 2015) Ref: 150106. Available at: https://www.gov.uk/government/publications/key-stage-3-the-wasted-years.
2 Ofsted and A. Spielman, HMCI Commentary: Curriculum and the New Education Inspection Framework (18 September 2018). Available at: https://www.gov.uk/government/speeches/hmci-commentary-curriculum-and-the-new-education-inspection-framework.

beginning in Year 7.[3] In the same survey, 53% of respondents claimed that the number of subjects on offer at GCSE level was also reducing, leading to concerns that education for 11–16-year-olds was becoming impoverished. These behaviours are predicated for the most part not on a genuine belief that getting exam results is the most important element of the education system, but the fear that this is the basis on which schools are judged and on which careers are made and broken. Remember that minister so desperate to make their mark that they put apples on the curriculum?

Human fallibility, stemming from a fear of failure coupled with ambition, runs like a crack through all levels of the system. It is a brave leader or teacher who avoids that chasm. Test results have become synonymous with survival, and this has placed great pressure on children who carry not only the responsibility for their own future but that of their teachers and school leaders too. Dealing with that pressure by teaching to the test, or pushing the test content down to younger children, is a grave error for all kinds of reasons. But we know why it happens. Any head teacher reading Peter Hyman's words on page 51 will know the excruciating stress of that system and the warp it creates.

The system used by Ofqual in England means that results for GCSE are set using a type of norm-referencing called comparable outcomes. In effect, this means that there is an expectation that the exam results of 16-year-olds will be roughly in line with their achievements at age 11. Broadly, this means that for one child to outperform expectations, another has to fail; for one school to achieve highly on the Progress 8 measure currently being used to judge a school's performance in England, another has to fall behind.

This linear progress data has many obvious flaws and unintended consequences, but none more damning than the impact it has had on the behaviour of some schools. A three-year GCSE programme is one such consequence, but there are also attempts by some to change the demographic of their school by 'encouraging' some children to leave and others to join. Massaging the figures in this way allows schools to buck trends on linear data because individuals are not tracked, merely cohorts. It would be possible for a low-attaining group of pupils to be off-rolled

3   J. Staufenberg, Half of Schools Start GCSEs in Year 9, NFER Survey Suggests, *Schools Week* (12 April 2019). Available at: https://schoolsweek.co.uk/half-of-schools-start-gcses-in-year-9-nfer-survey-suggests.

and replaced with higher attaining pupils, or not replaced at all, in order to manipulate outcomes – and, indeed, this does seem to be happening across the country. One survey by the Education Policy Institute found that 49,000 pupils had disappeared without explanation from the school roll in England, representing 8.1% of the total school population.[4]

The panic over end-point data and accountability has driven some schools into a moral cesspit of gaming. And it's no use Ofsted stepping up (finally) to condemn it when they have been part of the problem for so long. Until the government starts to recognise the mathematical impossibility of insisting on a policy of improvement in a system designed to keep things the same, some schools will continue to go mad. But not all.

Let's go back in time for a moment …

In 2004 the school I began describing at the beginning of this book was working to a slightly different GCSE measure – the five A*–C grades including English and maths measure. For readers teaching outside the English system, this measured school effectiveness by expecting that students would achieve five good passes including two in English and maths. Of course, this in itself led to some odd behaviours around what counted as a GCSE and how much effort staff put into borderline students at the expense of those who might have been challenged more but who were either secure or deemed to be lost causes.

Our school had a head teacher who was determined to do neither. He was of the firm belief that the answer to Key Stage 4 examination results lay in the quality of provision in Key Stage 3, and he was right. He believed that three things were necessary for this and much broader educational outcomes: improving oracy, developing a love of reading and placing children in deep contexts that would develop their humanity. Speaking in 2005, he stated: 'We are seeking to transform the child's experience in school and create a curriculum and assessment process that genuinely nurtures human development and enables young people to come to terms with who they are and how they relate to others.'[5]

....

4 S. Weale, More Than 49,000 Pupils 'Disappeared' from English Schools – Study, *The Guardian* (18 April 2019). Available at: https://www.theguardian.com/education/2019/apr/18/more-than-49000-pupils-disappeared-from-schools-study

5 Matthew Milburn quoted in D. Kidd, Assessment As an Act of Love, *Teaching Times* 1.1 (2005): 33–37 at 33. Available at: https://library.teachingtimes.com/articles/assessment-as-an-act-of-love.

As part of that vision, we created a Year 7 transition curriculum that combined the humanities subjects with English and drama to create 'cultural studies'. The stuff of nightmares for some, perhaps – but for us, a means by which children could use books as portals to the world, enhancing their understanding, building effective and connected schemas, and becoming articulate and confident learners in the process. At the end of the first year, the students were expected to write an extended philosophical essay of 1,500 words.

'They don't need that for GCSE!' commented one sceptical teacher. We weren't preparing them for GCSE, though; we were preparing them for an adult life in which they might need to produce an extended piece of writing, and for an 11-year-old life in which they might have something to say on a matter of importance to them.

At a time of three-part lessons, national strategies, tightly structured literacy sessions and the expectation that learning objectives would be writ large on boards, it was a risk to throw all that away and instead have lesson plans and learning pathways with big questions leading the way. But we didn't sacrifice knowledge, we enhanced it. When studying the Gunpowder Plot as part of a bigger unit of work around 'Plots and protests – how can we use our voices to change the world?', the children made connections between types of protest – linking 1605 to 2005; comparing the Catholic plot to modern-day terrorism; linking the Bishnoi Chipko movement in the 1700s to Rosa Parks and Martin Luther King; examining the motivations and actions of protest and considering which are most effective in achieving their aims; all the while looking at wider philosophical, ethical and religious frameworks so that the 'then' time connects to the 'now' time, the them to us. This is curriculum built around linking concepts – something central to the International Baccalaureate, for example.

In 2005 the percentage of students at the school gaining five A*–C grades including English and maths was 33%. By the time this cohort of students reached Year 11 it had risen by well over 20%. Improvements like this rarely happen in isolation to other interventions and strategies; nevertheless, the extended writing, deeper thinking and more active pedagogies employed by staff had a tangible quantifiable impact. In addition, qualitative research by Dr Elaine Millard showed gains in softer skills too – in children's confidence, engagement with the wider world around them, in whole-class inclusive teaching practices and in pupils being motivated to take direct action both in and out of school.[6] It seemed possible for a brief moment in time that one might have one's cake and eat it.

Of course, by then there had been a change of government, of mood and of ideology, and along came Michael Gove, cake-catcher, with a new national curriculum and a new set of priorities. Nevertheless, this experience deepened my belief that success in Key Stage 4 lies in investment in Key Stage 3 through a broad, relevant and challenging curriculum. In too many schools, curriculum has become synonymous with the test, as Ofsted have belatedly recognised:

> It seems unlikely that any school has prioritised testing over the curriculum as a deliberate choice. It is likely that, in some quarters, testing has come inadvertently to mean the curriculum in its entirety. If it is true that curriculum knowledge has weakened across the sector over time, it would explain why there has been a merging of the concepts of testing and the curriculum. If this is the case, it is despite the concerted efforts of the Department for Education (DfE) to make performance measures more nuanced, with the development of Progress 8 and the EBacc, for example. Inspection may well have unintentionally contributed to the shift by reinforcing the focus on measures. Measures only ever provide a partial picture: inspection should complement, not duplicate, that picture.[7]

Although we already know that the merest mention of curriculum from Ofsted can send the English education system into a panic, from which no doubt a hundred off-the-shelf packages will emerge, the conversation around what it is we want young people to learn – and perhaps more critically, how they learn it – is to be welcomed. But it is not new. It is a question that was being asked in the 1990s and early 2000s. Mick Waters outlines the three steps of thinking about curriculum that could easily now be seen as intention, implementation and impact:

6 M. Fautley, E. Millard and R. Hatcher, *Remaking the Curriculum: Re-engaging Young People in Secondary School* (Stoke-on-Trent: Trentham Books, 2011).

7 Ofsted and Spielman, HMCI's Commentary: Recent Primary and Secondary Curriculum Research.

1. What are we trying to achieve?
2. How do we organise learning?
3. How well are we achieving our aims?[8]

Nor is this the first time that Ofsted has mentioned the importance of curriculum. Take this from the 2012 (now archived) outstanding grade descriptors cited by Waters:

> [the curriculum] provides highly positive, memorable experiences and rich opportunities for high quality learning, has a positive impact on pupil's behaviour and safety and contributes well to pupil's achievements in their social, moral, spiritual and cultural development.[9]

The language of the new framework shifts away from this more emotive expectation of positivity, but teachers are nevertheless expected to 'create an environment that allows the learner to focus on learning',[10] and to do so in a way that makes learning connect to deeper conceptual understanding.

Whether Ofsted intended to remove the idea that children should actually enjoy learning doesn't matter; the fact remains that children who are emotionally invested in their learning and who experience learning positively are more likely to do well, as we see in the example on pages 59–62, in which Year 8 students take on the role of emergency aid workers. Moreover, a curriculum that is designed to place creativity, compassion and community on an equal footing to coherence and credibility is not in conflict with the framework but working within it.

8 Waters, *Thinking Allowed*, p. 273. See also: Ofsted, *An Investigation into How to Assess the Quality of Education Through Curriculum Intent, Implementation and Impact* (December 2018). Ref: 180035. Available at: https://www.gov.uk/government/publications/curriculum-research-assessing-intent-implementation-and-impact.

9 Waters, *Thinking Allowed*, p. 269.

10 Ofsted, *The Education Inspection Framework* (January 2019). Ref: 180039, p. 11. Available at: https://assets.publishing.service.gov.uk/government/uploads/system/uploads/attachment_data/file/801581/Proposed_Education_Inspection_Framework_draft_for_consultation_140119_archived.pdf.

Were we to apply the five pillars of curriculum design to the official commentaries on the new Ofsted Inspection Framework, we would see elements of each one emerging:

1. **Coherence:** 'the provider's curriculum is coherently planned and sequenced towards cumulatively sufficient knowledge and skills for future learning and employment' (p. 11).

2. **Credibility:** 'learners develop detailed knowledge and skills across the curriculum and, as a result, achieve well' (p. 12).

3. **Creativity:** Only joking – of course Ofsted doesn't mention creativity! But it does insist that 'the curriculum extends beyond the academic, technical or vocational and provides for learners' broader development, enabling them to develop and discover their interests and talents' (p. 12), and that 'teaching is designed to help learners to remember in the long term the content they have been taught and to integrate new knowledge into larger concepts' (p. 11).

4. **Compassion:** 'equipping them to be responsible, respectful, active citizens who contribute positively to society' (pp. 12–13).

5. **Community:** 'leaders engage effectively with learners and others in their community, including – where relevant – parents, carers, employers and local services ' (p. 13) and references to 'cultural capital' (p. 10).

In my opinion, Ofsted does not go far enough – but perhaps it's not their place to do so. Responsibility for setting the weather on curriculum lies with departments for education, although the enacted experience on the ground will always rest with teachers. In any case, if we have learned one thing over the past couple of decades it is that the framework will change again soon enough. For this reason alone we cannot plan for Ofsted; we need to plan for children. Under this framework there are too few references to community and to the kind of cultural capital to be gained through trips, experiences and collaborations; there is too little emphasis on the deep thinking of connected and creative processes; and too little mention of the well-being of children beyond basic safeguarding. Ofsted have made a step in the right direction, but many are way ahead in the field – both here and abroad – and have been for some time.

We've decided to shake up Year 8 a bit. English, maths and science together. What on earth could we have in common? We're sitting in a meeting planning a project funded by Creative Partnerships, a national project set up by the last Labour government to encourage collaboration between arts organisations and schools to build cultural capital and creativity in education. So here we are. I'm an English and drama secondary specialist with primary experience, but by no means familiar with secondary maths and science study, and I'm a bit nervous.

'They're doing instructions and writing to inform in English.'

'Data handling in maths.'

'We're doing waterborne diseases,' chips in science.

Who in the world might need to know all that? We ponder, and then it hits us.

- The earthquake in Haiti.
- A million refugees living under tarpaulin with no sanitary facilities.
- Ditches of sewage scarring the hillside.
- The rainy season approaching.

And we're off …

Let's say they are trainee emergency aid agency workers who need to figure out how to warn and protect the Haitian refugees from what the World Health Organization is describing as an impending catastrophe. How could we use writing and data to educate the refugees and the emergency aid workers on the ground about the dangers?

We decide to trial it with a couple of classes and see how it goes. When the students come to the first session we set out the story, the problem and the challenge. They are up for working as if they were in an emergency aid agency. They decide on a name and apply for their jobs, imagining themselves into a future in which they might have such responsibilities. Most have written CVs including GCSEs, A levels, degrees and relevant work experience. Mostly science related. Mostly.

'Hollywood actress,' writes one.

'Soldier,' writes another.

'OK – well, celebrity endorsements are always effective for our fundraising – thank you for giving up your time to join the team,' we say to one.

'Afghanistan? Well, you'll be highly experienced at logistics. Welcome aboard!' we say to the other. No child is irrelevant.

For the next few weeks, when they go to science they are entering the 'Centre for Disease Control' to learn the knowledge they will need to fulfil their professional duties. In English they are coming to a PR agency to be trained on how to communicate effectively, and we are layering in a fundraising element too. In maths, at the 'Office of National Statistics', they are looking at how the information they are finding out can be communicated in ways that are visually interesting and easy to understand – how data is presented to the wider public. Crucially, the teachers in each subject are working within their area of expertise and adopting the role of the expert. Because they are.

We notice three things early on:

1. Language is heightened. The students are grasping for vocabulary that they think professional adults would use. It makes it easy for us to layer that tier 2 vocabulary into the learning in a natural way.

2. Behaviour is being managed by peers. 'Don't be unprofessional – and crack on. We're Skyping the UN in 40 minutes – we'd better be ready!' said one usually quiet girl to the boy attempting to distract her.

3. They don't want it to stop. We are bombarded with requests to work through breaks, lunches and after school. The students are bringing in wider reading. They are watching the news and documentaries about Haiti at home. They are bringing in newspaper articles. They are a little obsessed.

Fast forward six weeks and they are presenting to a panel of visitors who have adopted the roles of members of the UN. The students know we are in a fiction – they recognise the head teacher and chair of governors – but they present earnestly and with great seriousness. They bring some surprises too. Some of the class are presenting their texts in French. When asked why, one student shrugs and says, 'That's what they speak in Haiti – we looked it up and translated it.'

Another child brings in a text consisting entirely of images and number data – almost like a cartoon. It's beautiful and informative but I'm going to struggle to assess it for English content. I ask her why.

'Haiti has a very high illiteracy rate,' she explains before pulling out another document. 'This one is for those who can read.'

So bothered are they that they don't want to stop at simply communicating their learning. They want to make a difference. And so they organise, in their own time, fundraising events for the people of Haiti – driven to be of service to the world. The unit combines all five aspects of the kind of curriculum design set out in this book. There is *coherence* across three major subject areas, while each one has maintained its own integrity. There is the *credibility* of knowledge. The pupils are being asked to find *creative* solutions to real-life problems – returning to the Haberman quote at the start of this book that 'living is a constant messing with problems that seem to resist solution'; they understand that there are no easy solutions to Haiti's problems but are willing to grapple with the difficulty regardless. They are demonstrating *compassion* to those who are suffering but in an active and solution-focused way so that their empathy leads to affirmative action, and for that they actively involve the *community* in fundraising. Nothing is lost in this approach from what might ordinarily have been taught. It has taken no more lesson time (although it did demand more student time and more meeting time for staff). But so much has been gained.

'Is that a top set?' asks a visitor of one group.

No. They were all mixed ability but you would never have guessed. Every child taking part, all with something to say.

Fast forward to the end-of-year tests. Our Haiti groups outperform the rest of the year, controlling for entry-point data from SATs. And teachers report that they seem more alert, more engaged, more interested and more articulate than other groups, even in unrelated subjects.

So did it last? Of course not. Cake-catcher and all that, but these things are possible. They are and always were possible. We just need to be brave. Dandelion-minded.

Planning for coherence in the Key Stage 3 or middle school curriculum doesn't mean that we either completely protect subject integrity or move towards a wholescale interdisciplinary way of working. It means that we look for echoes and strands that will strengthen a student's understanding. Here are ten examples of echoes of coherence that are possible in the secondary (or indeed any) curriculum:

1. Responding to a current event in the moment. When the Haiti earthquake occurred, a geography teacher shrugged and said, 'We don't do that until Year 9.' English, science and maths embraced it in the here and now.

2. If the English team are studying Shakespeare or the *Iliad* or Wilfred Owen, what are the history team teaching (and vice versa)? One of the most common complaints of English professors at university is their students' lack of contextual knowledge of literary texts. If they are studying 19th century literature, for example, are they studying Darwin in science?

3. Where is the curriculum in your local community? Do your humanities teams connect to explore local geography, history, religious buildings and businesses under one theme of 'our community'? How might PE connect to this?

4. If students are being asked to make something (food, a box, an app) in a subject like design and technology, art or computing, what opportunities are there for their object to link to a poem/be in a refugee survival pack/impact on climate change/help the homeless/meet the brief for a revision pack or learning resource/be exhibited in a local space? Do teachers in one subject know what is being taught in others so they can loop in where they see connections? Have you allocated continuing professional development (CPD) and meeting times for this kind of curriculum mapping to take place?

5. How does each one of your subjects utilise and build on links in the community? How many experts from outside school come in to speak with students? Do you know what all your students' parents have as a specialism – either through work or hobbies? Over the years we have encountered professors, heads of charities and business leaders, but also a magician, writer, fisherman, expert on ancient coins, carer for the terminally ill, gardener and keeper of snakes.

6. Do you allow students to learn outside the classroom? Did you let them watch an eclipse? Collect snow/bugs/flora and carry out observations and experiments? Are these observations shared with English to stimulate writing? Where are the patterns of nature in maths? How might science and maths and art combine under this common theme?

7. How many opportunities do students have to share their learning in other subjects through interpreting them in art and performance? Do your performing and visual arts teams talk to other subject teams to gather ideas for generating and creating artwork? Just think about how powerful this might be in terms of embedding and interpreting knowledge.

8. How many of your assessment processes allow a student to stand up and talk with their teachers, parents and peers together about what they have learned? Can students articulate their learning confidently to strangers? Is feedback a one-way street in your school?

9. How do past events link to current events? If history is teaching the Norman Conquest, is English looking at the impact on the etymology of our language? Is geography looking at how topography influences the outcomes of battles and

patterns of migration? Is science wrapping forces into a story about an arrow?

10. Are students learning that all we know in this world is connected to other knowing? That it is connected to the past and the future? That it is a tapestry as rich as the Earth itself and still being woven, so they are the threads and seams of the future? Does your curriculum offer hope through the weaving of these golden threads?

Chapter 5

The Unique Lives of Adolescents

(aka Gardening in Potentially Hostile Environments)

At Saddleworth School in Oldham, the school timetable collapses for four days every July in order to allow all students in Years 7–10 to take part in what is called the 'pupil-driven review' or PDR process. Over the four days, the students take part in PDR on an allocated day, have a day at home (an INSET allocation), and take part in a sports day and an arts day. It's a big logistical undertaking, but it allows for every student in the school to get their one hour of time in which they, their parents, a teacher and four peers really examine their learning over the year.

The students are expected to prepare a 15-minute presentation in advance. For those who feel, for whatever reason, that they can't stand and present for this length of time, they can make some artwork or a film, or produce texts to be read to fill the time and communicate what it is they need to say. A child with additional needs may present with a teaching assistant. But every student is expected to produce something that reflects on who they are, what they have learned and what they need to develop as they move forward. At the end of the 15 minutes there is a questioning and reporting session from their peers. The peers will comment on their observations of the student over the year and their thoughts about the presentation, and they will ask any questions they think are pertinent. They are well-prepared and taught how to offer constructive feedback. At that point the peers leave the room (activities are set up for them in the library throughout the day), and the student spends the final half hour with their parents and teacher, exploring the child's data, progress, punctuality, attendance and other issues.

There is an opportunity for a deep conversation about concerns. The session ends with targets being set which will be revisited in the following year's PDR.

One student, explaining the process, gave away perhaps more than they intended when they said: 'There's nowhere to hide. Your parents know what you're like at home. Your teacher and your classmates know what you're like at school. You can't really lie about how hard you're working because someone will catch you out!'

Parents also seem to value the time spent, with 90% of them reporting in evaluations that they found the process worthwhile. As one parent put it: 'I feel relieved, proud and confident that she will get good back-up at school. Full of respect for her tutor. Proud that Saddleworth School uses very valuable time to focus so individually on children.'

There are no grades in this process – no passes or fails. It's about students being offered the opportunity to have a voice about their learning and to share their interests, ambitions and hopes with the school community. Some students reflect more on their learning out of school. Some talk about the problems they have had settling in or making friends. Some talk about their struggles in certain subjects. In all cases there is a chance to consider, 'What are we going to do about that, together?' and this can be no bad thing. It's an example of how schools can move away from test scores and achievement data, flight paths and trackers, and towards a more individualised, constructive and humane process of assessment that bonds the community together.

The executive head teacher, Matthew Milburn, who devised the assessment process to sit alongside the 'humanising' curriculum model that he developed at his previous school in Barnsley, feels strongly that giving students opportunities to shape the conversations around their learning is a vital part in setting them off towards self-regulation and independence. There is also an additional impact on relationships at this fraught time of adolescence. When the system was first developed in Barnsley in 2009, I wrote an article about observing the process in action. I witnessed the following conversation between these students (names changed). The teacher had organised the peer feedback into critical and constructive friends, with a task allocated to the critical friend to find areas for improvement and the constructive friend to find things to praise.

Teacher: So how do you think Jordan has performed in terms of making friends and working in teams?

Critical friend: Well, it's quite hard to say this, but it's not just me who thinks it, but you mess around a lot and it's hard to concentrate when you're in our group because you distract everyone and that gets annoying.

Jordan's shoulders slump. He looks down.

Constructive friend: That's true, but I've been trying to work out why you're like that and I think that you don't have a lot of confidence in your work, so you mess about instead so people won't know. But you should have confidence, because you have some good ideas and you can be funny …

Critical friend: Yeah, you can.

Constructive friend: And so we think, don't we, that you should try to have more confidence and trust us to listen to your ideas because then you'll see that you can work well and you'll be better in a group.

Jordan sits up straighter. His head comes up. He smiles.[1]

It's a simple example of how powerful peer feedback can be to a student. Imagine, for example, if a teacher or parent had said these things – would they have had the same impact? Opening up opportunities for these gentle conversations in the planning around curriculum and assessment can be highly impactful. And it matters. We know from the work of Sarah-Jayne Blakemore how significant the impact of peer approval and acceptance is on the adolescent brain.[2] And David Hargreaves, writing in 2008, reminds us of the importance of attending to the emotional and social needs of adolescents in our assessment and curriculum: 'Our deepest needs concern how we relate to others.' He goes on to cite Avner Offer, who claims that we need the three A's – 'attention, affirmation and approbation':

Adolescents feel such needs acutely: for them there can be no well-being if they remain unmet. It is from their peers that they are most demanded. Many disadvantaged youngsters leave school with as superficial a grasp of friendship as of the curriculum subjects. Many need help to deal with their deep

---

1 See D. Kidd, Assessment As an Act of Love, 37.
2 S-J. Blakemore, *Inventing Ourselves: The Secret Life of the Teenage Brain* (New York: Doubleday, 2018).

fears of being rejected, humiliated and excluded by peers, and to overcome their conviction that friendship lies in rigid and shallow conformity to peer pressure, fashions and status hierarchies or in the dreams of the cult of celebrity.[3]

Hargreaves argues for a return to a 'moral' education which promotes well-being as 'a way of life rather than a state of mind'[4] and offers many examples from philosophy and psychology to show how this is important to the well-being of society. He argues that happiness in education is found in friendships, in purpose and in endeavour in which:

- frustration and hard work are inescapable elements;
- these are more bearable because they are shared with others;
- signature strengths are shared and valued by others.[5]

If we are to truly have a curriculum of hope in the English secondary school (or, indeed, anywhere else), we must attend to the emotional and social needs of adolescent learners as well as our cognitive expectations of them. Blakemore points out that adolescents are deeply attuned to feelings of shame and embarrassment, particularly around their peer group, and this might well impact on how we consider curriculum, assessment and pedagogy. While Hargreaves' work and that of cognitive scientists such as Sarah Michaels, Catherine O'Connor and Lauren Resnick, in their structured approach to group work through 'accountable talk',[6] suggests that group and project work can help young people in their academic achievements, all teachers know that this kind of work is not always easy to pull off in the classroom. That doesn't mean we shouldn't try. What kind

3   D. Hargreaves, *Deep Learning – 2: Why Should They Learn?* (London: Specialist Schools and Academies Trust, 2008), p. 43. See also: A. Offer, *The Challenge of Affluence: Self-Control and Well-Being in the United States and Britain since 1950* (New York: Oxford University Press, 2006).

4   Hargreaves, *Deep Learning*, p. 19.

5   Hargreaves, *Deep Learning*, p. 44.

6   S. Michaels, C. O'Connor and L. B. Resnick, Deliberative Discourse Idealized and Realized: Accountable Talk in the Classroom and in Civic Life, *Studies in Philosophy and Education* 27(4) (2008): 283–297.

of role models are we if we tell our young learners to avoid things that aren't easy and require practice and skill?

In 2016 I had the pleasure of visiting School 21 in London to see for myself the process underpinning its philosophy around rooting the curriculum in oracy, a pride in creating beautiful work and fostering strong independence and responsibility in children. The mission statement around the school was simple and effective: 'To create beautiful work that makes a difference to the world.'

Ron Berger's 'ethics of excellence'[7] are not simply talked about in this school; they are plastered all over the walls in the drafts and redrafts of children's work – right through from reception. Exhibits in which mistakes and corrections are as worthy of display as final products.

In the hall was an area labelled the 'War and Conflict Zone' and inside it sat two huge chess tables. Each chess piece was a sculpture created by Year 9 students who had been exploring the Cold War. During project-based learning, they examined the key players in the Cold War, researched them and created a chess piece to represent them. They then argued, debated and reached a consensus about who was who. What was the king? A pawn? A castle? Why? Their understanding was extraordinarily sophisticated.

Head of project-based learning Joe Pardoe was at pains to explain that the work in the school recognised the importance of knowledge, but also felt that our education system is predicated on an assumption that the children don't know until we tell them – what he called 'a pre-emptive system'. He gave several examples of where this world view had been shaken by his students – those who could speak Russian and who brought so much to a project on the Russian Revolution, or one who brought in prior knowledge of Rousseau when they were exploring the French Revolution. 'It's so much better to start with what they already know and work from there,' he said. Simple and obvious. Why don't we all do it? Well, you need three things – time, structure and purpose.

On the walls of the project-based learning area were clear targets, deadlines and goals. 'Creativity operates within constraints,' he explained, 'deadlines, briefs,

---

7   R. Berger, *An Ethic of Excellence: Building a Culture of Craftsmanship with Students* (Portsmouth, NH: Heinemann, 2003).

obstacles …' So, while the children are given creative briefs, they exist within tight and demanding constraints.

The structure of how the lessons operate was explicit. They started each 100-minute session with a 20-minute lecture – Joe observed that 'there is a place for the didactic and for teacher talk'. On the board was written 'University-style lecture'. It was clear that the routines of higher education were writ large in the minds of everyone involved. Underneath was written 'University-style seminars', and during the lesson the students were withdrawn, 12 at a time, to work with a member of staff in response to a text they were given to read in advance. Flipped learning, you might call it. The rest of the time was given over to individual project work, with Joe circulating and offering feedback to students.

'In an average lesson, I probably get to spend three minutes one to one with each pupil – it's not much,' he shrugs. But it's more than most teachers can say, and even just a couple of minutes of targeted, personal verbal feedback can significantly affect learning outcomes, particularly when the feedback allows for freely constructed responses.[8]

As Peter Hyman explains: 'Interdisciplinary work is another way in which subject knowledge can be applied with real purpose. Pupils should be able to use their knowledge in two or more subject disciplines to shed light on a problem.'[9] No one could accuse this school of tenuous cross-curricular practice. It is careful and considered. It is coherent.

When I wrote in the introduction about the curriculum demonstrating compassion towards young people, these were the kinds of processes I had in mind. Happiness for all humans is deeply rooted in a sense of purpose, but for adolescents shared purpose and experience are particularly potent. It is important for us to consider how the curriculum either imposes additional pressure on or supports the well-being of these learners at a vulnerable stage of development. These signature strengths are set out in the work of Martin Seligman, who lists the core qualities which best equip people for 'authentic happiness' as:

8   See R. Lyster and K. Saito, Oral Feedback in Classroom SLA: A Meta-Analysis, *Studies in Second Language Acquisition* 32(2) (2010): 365–302.
9   Hyman, A Curriculum of Head, Heart and Hand.

- Wisdom and knowledge (e.g. curiosity, love of learning, open-mindedness, ingenuity, perspective).

- Courage (e.g. bravery, diligence, integrity).

- Humanity and love (e.g. kindness, accepting love, loving oneself).

- Justice (e.g. duty, teamwork, fairness, leadership).

- Temperance (e.g. self-control, discretion, humility).

- Transcendence (e.g. appreciation of beauty and excellence, gratitude, hope, playfulness).[10]

It seems to me to be entirely possible to develop a curriculum that helps adolescents to practise and experience these states of being without significantly impacting on workload for teachers by simply creating deep and purposeful contexts for learning and broader and more humane means of assessing that learning. This is not a matter of a skills vs. knowledge model, and nor is it about loading more and more onto ever wearier teachers. It is a matter of imbuing the curriculum with meaning and opportunity.

What the examples in this chapter show us is that it is entirely possible, even within the rigid constraints of the English education system, to develop meaningful learning for children in early adolescence (11–14): learning which makes them think deeply, is broad and purposeful, engages their creativity and compassion and allows them to be freed from the tyranny of external examinations, while developing all the habits of mind, language, socialisation and discipline that will support that study when the time comes.

Nowhere is it more challenging to do this than in an alternative provision setting with a transient and sometimes damaged school population. Yet many of these schools are managing to do just that. From Springwell alternative provision academies across Yorkshire and Humberside to the small Kingsland pupil referral unit in Oldham, changes are being made to the curriculum to make learning meaningful and engaging to young people.

At Kingsland school, we have just launched the new curriculum for Key Stage 3. Classes can include students from all three year groups at Key Stage 3 as well as

---

10 M. E. P. Seligman, *Authentic Happiness: Using the New Positive Psychology to Realize Your Potential for Lasting Fulfillment* (New York: Free Press, 2002).

having to cope with the students being in school sometimes for just a few weeks, sometimes for months, sometimes permanently and sometimes hardly at all. These are young people with nowhere left to go, but the school does not give up on them. We are in the process of planning a three-year rolling curriculum programme which will weave various subjects together, while keeping maths separate (although allowing for skills being developed in maths to be practised in context). Our first unit is 'A Mission to Mars'. The teachers are fully aware of how tightly they need to anchor lessons, but they are led by warm and strong relationships, which take priority over everything else.

The class I'm observing are hoping to be reintegrated back into mainstream education soon. They are curious about the Mars mission and engaged in thinking about who we should take with us. They have worked through some knowledge, including misconceptions about the solar system, and they have had some of their questions answered with regard to the science: why is it hotter in some places on Earth than others? What is an atmosphere? Why isn't Mercury hotter than Venus when it's closer to the sun? ('That's sly, that!')

We're dealing with edgy kids but curious minds, so they don't always ask questions in the ways we might expect:

Student A: Ey, no way is that a star – look at the size of it. Stars are little – tell him, Sir – there's no way the sun is a star! It's a sun!

And some of their answers are colourful too:

Student A: What if someone has a baby up there – will it adapt?

Teacher: Adapt?

Student A: Yeah – to gravity and that.

Teacher: Well, real adaptations – if we're thinking of evolution – take tens of thousands of years, but it would adapt to a lower force of gravity, yes.

Student B: It'll be fucking massive!

Teacher: Taller perhaps, yes.

Of course the teacher addresses the language issue, quietly and discreetly, but these are young people who find it hard to stay in their seats. To be sufficiently interested to grapple with questions about gravity, adaptations and space is a win.

The unit of work emerged from a primary unit that we will explore in Chapter 8, but these teachers have anchored it into a progression of tasks and areas of learning that allow the students to plait the more difficult personal, social, health and economic (PSHE) knowledge they need into the work on space. For example, one of the teachers is concerned about the level of drug taking that some of the students seem to think is 'normal'. A great deal of work is being done across the school, in partnership with other local services, to try to tackle this issue, but it doesn't always get through.

These students, as employees of NASA, are charged with the responsibility of recruiting a team to build a colony on Mars. They have selected the team, interviewed them and called the candidates to break the news of whether or not they have been successful (with willing teachers and teaching assistants on the other end of the 'phone'). This has enabled them to think about the process of applying for jobs, the kinds of qualities an employer might look for and the types of questions that might be asked in an interview. They have taken to this positively and have undertaken their responsibilities seriously, so we weave in an additional element. They get a letter from the HR department:

Thank you for selecting the applicants for the Mission to Mars. We now need to proceed with a number of medical and security checks before training can begin. Please inform the candidates that they will need to bring some identification along to their fitness and drug tests as part of their induction meeting.

The letter is building vocabulary, but it also does something more important. It gently reminds the students that out there in the world of work there will be checks and balances which hold them to account to standards of behaviour. They know this is a story, a fiction, and that there will be no real drugs test in school. But the point has been made, and the resulting conversation offers an opportunity to explore the issue further.

In this way, a unit that was designed initially for primary-age children is being adapted for the unique needs of older students, and adapted further for the needs of adolescents who have found themselves outside of the mainstream system. The process is mapped out carefully by teachers and summarised in their order of teaching:

1. Complete the letter to mum and dad – establishing people, place, problem (English).

2. Assemble the team – gathering resources and people (reading comprehension – English).

3. Why Mars? – training the team (science).

4. What do we know about our solar system? Orbits and planets? – training the team (science, non-fiction reading – English).

5. Creating displays (for the foyer) about the solar system (art and design).

6. Tackling misconceptions – training the team (science).

7. We want you – application processes (PSHE/English).

8. The history of space travel and international treaties – can we use these to provide inspiration to name our project/ship? (history)

9. Designing the ship (ICT/DT/maths/science).

10. Provisions – what are we taking and why? (science, geography, PSHE)

11. Creating a memory box – what will we take with us in order to remember Earth and the achievements of humankind? (art but also so much more)

12. Saying goodbye – letters and diaries (English).

13. The ship's log – keeping records (geography, English, science).

14. The arrival – building a settlement (geography, science, citizenship, PSHE).

15. Survival – shelter, plants and food (DT, geography, science).

16. Dilemma – new people coming – preparing to expand. Do we need a place of worship or are we going to be a secular society? Do we need a constitution? A bill of rights? Laws? Are we to be a democracy? (RE/citizenship)

17. Building a bigger community – a colony (history of colonisation, science).

18. A new dilemma – protests from Earth – why do we get to take over another planet when we have ruined this one? – link to the next unit on climate change …

....

In this example we see plaiting in action – it allows the students to weave their subjects into an overarching context. Subject knowledge is revisited several times and reading and writing are infused throughout. The students are also able to use other curriculum time to develop an interest in science fiction texts and to link their fictional contexts to news items about current projects in space. As numbers of staff are too small to facilitate the traditional subject specialist per subject approach you see in most secondary schools, this school has had to be more creative in its approach. However, those with subject specialisms are instrumental in creating the resources and mapping the content of their subject area onto the process.

We are in the early stages of this work, but the teachers are unanimous in their view that the students are paying more attention, staying in class more, extending their vocabulary and demonstrating an interest in knowing more and understanding more. There is no reason why more can't be done in mainstream secondary to achieve the same aims, and perhaps to assist in keeping some of these children in the mainstream system in the first place.

Chapter 6
A Curriculum for Wales
A Feathered Fledgling of Hope

We recognise that learning should be seen as similar to an expedition – with stops, detours and spurts.

Welsh Government (2019)[1]

In 2022 the new Curriculum for Wales comes into force after several years of pilots, tweaks and consultations. The aims of the curriculum, based on the recommendations of Graham Donaldson in his report of 2015, are fourfold:

- ambitious, capable learners, ready to learn throughout their lives
- enterprising, creative contributors, ready to play a full part in life and work
- ethical, informed citizens of Wales and the world
- healthy, confident individuals, ready to lead fulfilling lives as valued members of society.[2]

It is not unusual for a nation to set out grand statements for its curriculum aims, but what sets Wales apart from, say, England is the holistic approach it has taken in placing curriculum in a wider context by looking at the drivers for behaviour

---

1 See https://hwb.gov.wales/draft-curriculum-for-wales-2022/assessment-and-evaluation-framework/assessment-proposals.
2 G. Donaldson, *Successful Futures: Independent Review of Curriculum and Assessment Arrangements in Wales* (February) (Cardiff: Welsh Government, 2015), p. 29. Available at: https://gweddill.gov.wales/docs/dcells/publications/150225-successful-futures-en.pdf.

and change in schools. As such, there is a recognition that high-stakes, high-accountability testing has skewed the curriculum experience for children and that both assessment and inspection have to be reviewed in line with curriculum changes. In addition, they have taken their time. The journey from the initial report to the first implementation of the curriculum (for nursery to Year 7) will have taken seven years. There have been extensive pilots and consultations, and the Welsh government have made it clear that this is a long-haul change for the future – perhaps recognising that other successful systems, like Singapore and Finland, plan for the long term and not for short-term political churn.

There have been some knee-jerk criticisms of the curriculum already, with some seizing on the idea that the curriculum moves away from subjects towards 'areas of learning' as evidence of dumbing down. They also point to the teething problems of the Scottish Curriculum for Excellence as evidence that such models 'don't work'.[3] But they do a great disservice to the broad vision offered in the new curriculum, including the role that direct or explicit teaching has to play in the acquisition of knowledge.

In fact, the curriculum offers great scope to strengthen and develop schemas by understanding what connects subjects and allowing children to think in ways that are deeply knowledgeable and rooted in meaningful contexts. For example, a domain of engineering might well draw on a variety of subjects, such as maths, science, computing and design. An inquiry question such as, 'How did the ancients map the world?' might bring together history and anthropology with maths, science and geography, utilising knowledge from each to form conclusions and creating a broader schema of learning from which to draw upon in the future. What the Curriculum for Wales allows us to do is to find these touchpoints more easily, working not only within areas of learning and experience (AoLE) but also across them. This model lends itself beautifully to the notion of plaited planning outlined in Chapter 3; there are some examples of what this might look like in the appendix.

The Curriculum for Wales is designed to place ethics and health on an equal footing with academic achievement; it acknowledges the interdependence between the

....

3   G. Ashman, Bad Times Ahead for Education in Wales, *Filling the Pail* (24 March 2017) [blog]. Available at: https://gregashman.wordpress.com/2017/03/24/bad-times-ahead-for-education-in-wales. See also: https://scotlandscurriculum.scot.

cognitive, social and physical domains of learning. It forces a collaboration of sorts across subjects and between academic and pastoral care by not only grouping subjects into six areas of learning and experience (languages, literacy and communication; expressive arts; humanities; maths and numeracy; science and technology; health and well-being), but also having cross-AoLE competencies that unite them – numeracy, literacy, digital literacy and Welsh culture and language, as well as the health and well-being of children. The AoLEs offer an opportunity to find exactly the coherent links across the curriculum that Ofsted, over the border in England, is beginning to look for and which will strengthen schematic connections. (Note how experience in Wales is an entitlement and not just a vague reference to cultural capital.) Where are the crossovers between subjects? What ethical, global and social issues can unite us? How can children make connections between the things they learn so they can think more flexibly and creatively? How can they, in multi-sensory ways, directly experience their learning? These are opportunities and not restrictions.

Such innovations are nothing if the accountability and testing cultures which drive gaming and narrowing in schools are not addressed. While the Welsh government have made promising noises in this direction – for example, announcing that no testing in schools for national standards will be made public and calling off inspections to allow schools time to implement the curriculum – it remains to be seen whether schools will still be bound by these constraints.

Underpinning the new curriculum are 12 pedagogical principles that focus on a child's right to enquire, solve problems, collaborate and take ownership of their learning. But they also trust teachers to develop a 'blended' approach, choosing the methods that best suit their goals and making clear that there is a place for direct and explicit instruction in learning. There is a high level of teacher trust, scope for developing innovative practice and a belief that teachers and children together can become agents of change. But innovation requires knowledge and imagination, and inquiry is only as good as the question and scaffolding that supports it. Training will be essential if the curriculum is to live out its intentions.

One of the pilot schools testing out the new vision is Henry Tudor School in Pembroke. For the past two years, Hywel Roberts and I have been helping the school to design their curriculum for Years 7 and 8 so they are ready to hit the ground running not just in their pilot AoLE (humanities) but across the whole school. Under the guidance of assistant head Sarah Smith, the school has begun to develop a vision for their curriculum that is in tune with the national vision but also meets the specific needs of their local community. Blending international contexts with local ones (such as the *Sea Empress* oil spill), local tourism and conservation and the rich geography that Pembrokeshire has to offer, the school is crafting an exciting model for learning. Here Sarah outlines her intentions for the student experience:

Our Key Stage 3 curriculum is based around inquiry. Each faculty is developing inquiries that will confront our learners with ethical, authentic problems that will challenge them to engage with big questions that we face in today's world that have no easy answers: should the world have borders? Do we need to talk? Can a place be protected forever?

In doing this we hope our learners will become informed and ethical citizens, aware of the challenges that society faces, and equipped with the relevant knowledge and skills they need in the world, such as compassion, curiosity and the ability to work together to resolve complex current and future problems. We want to design a curriculum that is of relevance to their lives, rather than just of relevance to what is on the exam paper at the end of Year 11; a curriculum that looks out and connects with the world as it is now and as it can be, rather than one that reverses into the future.

When starting with aims such as these, it is important to think about what children need to know as well as what they need to do, and the school is committed to developing vocabulary and a love of reading across all areas of learning. As such, one autumn morning in 2017 we find ourselves planning a unit of work for humanities based on Katherine Rundell's book *The Explorer*. It's a brilliant text, encompassing a number of possible areas for learning. There is the obvious opportunity of the setting – the Amazon rainforest. There is an ancient city hidden in the forest jealously guarded by a mysterious explorer who intends to protect it from 'discovery'. There are themes around our responsibility for human and natural heritage coming into conflict with our desire for glory and recognition. There are themes of pushing past your limitations, trying new things and paying attention to what is around you. All of these are lessons worth learning in themselves: 'You don't have to be in a jungle to be an explorer … Every human on this earth is an explorer. Exploring is nothing more than the paying of attention, writ large. *Attention*. That's what the world asks of you.'[4]

The possibilities for learning that the book generates are rich and cut across all the humanities subject areas, but the students usually learn these subjects separately and some of the broader questions around how we live and how we learn from our past and present may well be lost. Under normal circumstances, they would be 'doing' the Black Death in history, Antarctica in geography, creation and ritual in RE, stakeholders in business and so on. How on earth can we get them to fit together through the reading of this book? We start to plait.

We begin with an overarching question: 'Would the world be better off without us?' And from this, the individual subject leaders generate inquiry questions that they think link this central question to their usual curriculum content and to the book.

- Business/IT: Can ecotourism ever really be ethical?

- Geography: Can a place be protected forever?

- History: Has exploration always been a good thing?

- RE: How do human beings make sense of their creation?

4 K. Rundell, *The Explorer* (London: Bloomsbury Children's Books, 2017), p. 255.

This allows us to connect to the book beautifully. We leave the Black Death behind a little and think more about how diseases were spread by Europeans to indigenous people, and how we might learn from this in order to ensure the safety of the tribal people in the forest. We think about how we might study the Antarctic Treaty and apply it to the development of a new one for the Amazon. We think about how ancient civilisations made sense of the world through creation stories and how these stories might be left as images in the ancient city. We think about what the implications might be for ethical business practice, if the site was to be accessed, whether local people would benefit and whether any kind of disturbance could be justified.

We ask, what if, in spite of all the promises of the children in the book, the outside world finds out about the hidden city? What would happen? What if we were a team commissioned to conduct a feasibility study into allowing people to access the site? What would be the opportunities and costs? What would the students recommend? Can we protect it forever?

All of these lenses offer students an opportunity not just to know (the factual information they will acquire is no less than they would have had before), but to think deeply about making connections between subject and real and imagined worlds. They are placed in the position not of being passive recipients of knowledge but active users of knowledge, so they can work their way through difficulty and consider the many ethical dilemmas that the development of this site would offer. The fact that they are being enticed into enjoying a book along the way is a happy but very important bonus.

Since that first unit was developed, innovative planning has been taking place across the school. Connections between and across AoLEs are emerging all the time. For example, maths had already started to think about the expectation in the curriculum that numeracy could link to well-being and had decided to work their data-handling unit around food and health. This led to a natural collaboration with the PE (or health and well-being) team. In addition to building skills in PE, they wanted to look at the impact of exercise on mental health. They intended to use questionnaires and information to get the students to consider this issue, so why not team up with maths to make this into a bigger project about nutrition and health without compromising on either subject's individual needs? It's just another layer of application. Once that idea had started to grow, there was no stopping the maths team. 'How did the ancients map the world?' turned our gaze towards the humanities. But the maths team would come at it from mapping angles in the constellations, looking at grid referencing, coordinates and patterns in nature. Redesigning an abandoned theme park brought them in close alignment with business, technology and science.

In languages and communication, the English, Welsh and Spanish departments came together and within minutes connections were being made. Suggestions to build on the existing triple literacy bonds they had (where each department agreed to look at points of grammar at the same time so the students could compare, for example, tenses across the three languages), led to them deciding to unite over the same text that the humanities team were using to explore migration – *The Arrival* by Shaun Tan.[5] There was no need to co-plan with the humanities team; the use of the same text creates an 'echo' across the curriculum, encouraging the students to make connections without unnecessary repetition.

In the text, the use of language to both engage and disengage human beings from communities is strongly explored. The idea of language as power is inherent throughout, and so it seemed like a good place for the English department to start. In the Welsh and Spanish classrooms, the students would use examples from the text of people struggling to communicate in a new place and would ask the question, 'When people arrive in an unfamiliar place, what are the most important things they need to ask and understand?' Vocabulary would be learned in response to the students' thoughts in this area. The wonderful librarian at the school sat in, making notes and suggesting that the students could make and listen to audio guides for visitors to new places. A collaboration between library, languages, communication and humanities started to emerge.

Science and technology are building their curriculum around three key ideas – understanding our planet, saving our planet and leaving our planet – and weaving all the necessary aspects of science and technology into these three areas, creating touchpoints in the day-to-day teaching of curriculum and in pull-down 'themed days' in which the students get to take part in practical experiments and make products that connect to the scientific concepts they are studying.

....

5   S. Tan, *The Arrival* (London: Hodder Children's Books, 2007).

In expressive arts (covering visual art, music, dance and drama), a whole year's worth of work was broken down into three termly themes under the umbrella question of 'What is art?':

- Term 1: art as resistance (protests and political art).

- Term 2: art as expression (identity and aesthetic).

- Term 3: art as reflection (society and the natural world).

For example, the work of the artist Hundertwasser gave us a starting point around art as expression. The notion of 'hiding in plain sight' takes on additional meaning when we learn about the life story of the artist. Hundertwasser and his mother avoided the Holocaust by hiding as Christians during the war. Baptised in 1935, protected from suspicion by the fact that his father was Christian and completing his disguise by joining the Hitler Youth, Hundertwasser grapples with identity and the notion of hiding in his art. The art department is rubbing shoulders with history but not imposing on history; this echoing is deliberately planned across the curriculum but not forced. The notion of hiding in plain sight could also be interrogated in other art forms as a means of exploring identity.

Underpinning it all is an ethical frame bound up with the idea that education should seek to empower students to be active citizens who will change the world, not simply exist within it. This purpose sits firmly at the heart of the new curriculum which makes explicit the duty of teaching as a means by which we don't simply create knowledgeable citizens, but also help children to become ethically informed, healthy, aspirational citizens of Wales and of the world. I know there will be cynics who sneer at such ambition, but not me. I embrace it, and it's wonderful to see staff and students at this school doing the same.

Two Year 5 classes at a primary school in Pembrokeshire. I'm teaching with Hywel Roberts. He has one class before lunch and I have the other class afterwards, so we think about how we can get them to connect. Their theme is 'Castles', and over dinner the night before we are considering how we can make this traditional topic model some of the principles embedded in the new Curriculum for Wales – without freaking out their teachers and making them think they have to rewrite everything from scratch. We need a way in. We put 'the history of Welsh castles' into a search engine and suddenly our portcullis has lifted and we have a way in. The year is 1409 and Margaret Hanmer, the wife of rebel leader Owain Glyndŵr, is facing the advancing army of Henry IV with her husband nowhere to be seen. Who are the people whose opinions we might consider here? We come up with two points of view: the people inside the castle and those on the outside – Margaret and her advisers and the Welsh farmers caught between the two.

In Hywel's class, the farmers consider how they might persuade Margaret to let them in. They know that a siege will require food, livestock and supplies and they can offer this. Equally, they know that an advancing English army is likely to take all of that from them. Time is of the essence and the children, as hopeful farmers, gather at the gate of the castle to make their plea. As Margaret is too busy to see them, they have to go away and submit their plea in writing. They go off to lunch.

Over lunch the two Year 5 classes have the gall to talk to one another, so when my class come in they are all abuzz about what is going on. But we are looking at the story from another angle.

Let's say we are in a castle in 1409, and in that castle there is a lady's chamber. What wouldn't it have in it? No PlayStation 4, no TV, no Domino's Pizza box … What might it have in it? The children stand in the room and describe objects to me. From velvet curtains to a four-poster bed, from jewels to a chamber pot. The lady in this room is worried. Her husband is leading a Welsh rebellion and she has not seen him for a long time. She thought she was safe, but a messenger arrived today with a frightening message. Would you like to talk to her? And they're off …

When they hear that an army is advancing – just days away – and that she doesn't think they have enough supplies to withstand a siege for long, the children get planning and making suggestions.

'My Lady, we should pray to God!'

(What might we say in that prayer?)

'My Lady, perhaps we should surrender and let them in and then the people might survive!'

(But what would my husband think?)

'My Lady, we must prepare for a siege and save our food and supplies.'

(What do we need to save? What have we got? How long will it last? Is the castle secure?)

'My Lady, I have a message from some farmers in the valley.'

Our Year 5 farmers are not best pleased when Margaret says she will take their food and livestock but only offer protection to the women and children – she says the men will have to fight.

We decide we need to know more about sieges and supplies in this period of history – how can we help Margaret and the farmers if we don't have this knowledge? And who is this king from England anyway, and what does he want with us?

We and us. The threads that bind then and now.

Planning for the Curriculum for Wales in primary schools should be simple if a plaited approach is adopted, and if bigger connected questions drive the thinking of curriculum planning. Taking a unit like 'Castles' and altering the focus to consider, 'How have castles played a part in Welsh history?' or 'Castles – traps or sanctuaries?' or 'How have human beings protected themselves from invasions through time?' allow for a broader focus to emerge and protect it from becoming a process of simply identifying and labelling parts of a castle and naming a few. A chance to visit a castle is even more interesting if the children have already placed a character from history there and taken a walk in her shoes. The interdependence of geography and history in castles is obvious, but there is also a world of language, ethics, values and justice to explore, books to read, texts to write.

If we take this example and think about the five pillars of planning, we can see how clearly they emerge:

1. **Coherence:** The unit links Welsh culture and history to the topic and connects chronologically and thematically to concepts around power, ownership and independence that will come up elsewhere in the curriculum.

2. **Credibility:** The children are being held accountable to facts – dates, names, events – and authentic details linked to the time period – from chamber pots to wells.

3. **Creativity:** The children are having to adapt their knowledge to shifting circumstances and come up with creative solutions to difficult problems.

4. **Compassion:** The children are having to consider multiple points of view and explore the impact of war and conflict on people.

5. **Community:** The children are learning about the history of a place of local interest, utilising the opportunity to visit the castle and develop a deeper understanding of their national culture. They will have an opportunity to learn from historians in the process.

Chapter 7

Exotic Plants

Tales from International Contexts

The International Baccalaureate aims to develop inquiring, knowledgeable and caring young people who help to create a better and more peaceful world through intercultural understanding and respect.

To this end the organization works with schools, governments and international organizations to develop challenging programmes of international education and rigorous assessment.

These programmes encourage students across the world to become active, compassionate and *lifelong learners who understand that other people, with their differences, can also be right.*

International Baccalaureate[1]

It is sometimes hard to conceptualise what a curriculum might look like without the political interference of politicians and without national interest shaping the values and content of the curriculum, and yet there is a quite unique example in existence in international schools – the International Baccalaureate (IB).

The IB was created in order to cater for the needs of families who may, in the course of a child's educational lifetime, live in several countries. Traditionally, parents who had to travel for work would have had a choice to either send their child to boarding school or to hope for the best in dragging them across several disconnected local systems. The IB allowed for a consistent programme of study from the Primary Years Programme through the Middle Years Programme to the IB Diploma, with the intention being that each could exist separately but that

---

1 See https://www.ibo.org/about-the-ib/mission (my emphasis).

together they would build the skills, attributes and knowledge to succeed at a higher level, whether students choose the academic diploma route or the more vocational Career-related Programme. In recent years many schools and governments have started to offer the IB for 16–19 provision as an option within their state systems.

The diploma course is internationally recognised as a system of excellence, and increasingly seen as a positive stepping stone into higher education and beyond.[2] In the UK it is frequently offered in private schools, although the government have indicated an intention to withdraw financial support for it in state schools.[3] Students are expected to study six subjects across Studies in Language and Literature, Language Acquisition, Individuals and Societies, Sciences, Mathematics and the Arts – and, in addition to examinations, they must also complete an extended essay, study 'The Theory of Knowledge' and take part in Creativity, Activity and Service (CAS) projects.

For the Primary and Middle Years Programmes, detail on content is limited, for reasons outlined below, and the focus is very much on developing attitudes, skills and competencies which develop the learner in preparation for the breadth of study at the higher levels. This can be delivered to varying degrees of success and there is a complex accreditation and moderation process to ensure a level of quality across the world. That's not to say that knowledge doesn't get taught – it does – but it is left to the discretion of the teacher to choose content that is suitable to the context – the country the school is in and the nationalities of the children in the class – and to leave room to be able to respond to current and cultural events.

Knowledge becomes complex and controversial in this type of educational system. If you are catering for a global population where a school community may have children hailing from 70 different countries, whose history do you teach? Which texts? The IB had to evolve to develop enough structure upon which to allow teachers to hang knowledge, but enough freedom for them to be able to tailor content to their particular school and community's needs. Not an easy task.

2 International Baccalaureate, Key Findings from Research on the Impact of the Diploma Programme (2016). Available at: https://www.ibo.org/globalassets/publications/become-an-ib-school/research-dp-findings-en.pdf.

3 P. Allen-Kinross, Withdrawing Funding from the IB Will Be a 'Tragedy' for Social Mobility, Heads Warn, *Schools Week* (18 May 2019). Available at: https://schoolsweek.co.uk/withdrawing-funding-from-the-ib-will-be-a-tragedy-for-social-mobility-heads-warn.

Sitting at the heart of the IB is the notion of 'international mindedness' and the idea that learning is a global endeavour. Learning across subject disciplines is linked through concepts and inquiry, and students are profiled according to learner attributes and capacities in what to many might simply look like a 'skills-based' curriculum, but in fact simply offers a structured framework on which a teacher and school can position knowledge. Indeed, knowledge is deeply embedded in the diploma, with students expected to study a range of subjects rather than specialising, as is the norm at A level. The diploma also explicitly requires students to work through uncertainty, to research, to consider ontological positions and to contribute to wider society.

However, as with any curriculum model, pedagogy is the key. No curriculum can properly succeed without high-quality teaching. That is not to say that children can't learn anything without a teacher – they clearly can – but a great curriculum is characterised by great teaching which leads to great outcomes. The teacher is the lynchpin which can spark innovative and thoughtful responses to curriculum.

At Island School in Hong Kong, I see students enthusiastically creating artwork around the school to show how art could function as social commentary. A Banksy-like panda bear clinging to a drain pipe above a water fountain. A small child positioned outside the library with balloons drifting away from her labelled 'money', 'food' and 'shelter', but with the word 'education' written on the balloon she still held in her hand. The teacher inspired.

At Nexus International School in Singapore, parents, children and teachers come together in the STEAM maker space on Saturday mornings to play and create together. I see young children engaged in their space topic, making holograms and using green-screen technology to create films to demonstrate their learning and owning every moment in the process. The teacher facilitated and guided.

At the International Community School of Addis Ababa, I see young politicians arguing cogently, and with the deep knowledge that comes from living in a place as economically polarised as theirs, about the complexities of foreign aid as part of their Model United Nations project. The teacher lit a flame.

In the International School of Brussels, I see children marching with their teachers to protest about climate change. The teacher stood in solidarity.

In Cambodia, students from the Western International School of Shanghai are working to rebuild a village, while also understanding the problems around imposing their cultural beliefs and values on others. The teacher questioned.

In Nanjing, I see children caring deeply about the disappearing natural habitat of giant pandas. They know facts and figures, they can make calculations and predictions. The teacher explained.

Teachers have to adopt and adapt their pedagogical stances to meet the needs of the students with whom they work, and in international settings, the social, cultural and linguistic can be multiply complex. Embracing those differences and celebrating them sits at the heart of the globally minded philosophy of the IB, as does student agency.

There is an inherent belief in the IB that students are capable partners in learning, which is exemplified beautifully in this extract from infant school teacher Rachael Mweti's blog about her teaching at Nexus International School in Singapore – an all-through IB school. She is exploring with her young charges the idea of being a scientist and has given them white coats to try on while they work (back to the Batman effect again). One of the things she notices is that with the lab coats on, being 'scientists', some of the girls are pretending to be men. She makes a mental note to challenge some stereotypes and begins to explore with the children what it means to think like a scientist rather than simply look like one.

As they removed the coats, I asked them, 'Are you still a scientist now you have taken the coat off?' It provoked some interesting responses, and I could pretty much sit back as they debated whether it was the coat that made them scientists, and if scientists were just a special type of person. We came up with a list of things scientists do – observe, experiment, come up with new ideas, test things, ask questions. 'Do you do those things?' I asked. They thought no, so I showed them the evidence. Pictures of them playing with toy cars and ramps, changing the angle, wondering if they could make it fly into a bucket, trying bigger cars, smaller cars. This was not something I had set up, just general classroom stuff. And they started to see it. That we are all scientists.

As the unit developed, we saw this more and more. … My little scientists were taking another step closer to realising they could be anything![4]

In her charming accounts of very young children making conceptual sense of the world, Rachael employs a number of stances. She will question, assess, provide information and resources, take on roles and teach from the front where necessary, but all with the aim of building a sense of learner identity and agency into the material to be learned.

This positioning allows her to thread unplanned diversions into the learning. She might choose to focus on women who are scientists in the world, linking broader issues around gender into the explorations of light and sound that the curriculum has planned. She will weave and adapt the needs of her particular class into the learning because that is what good teachers do, wherever they are.

It is not difficult to take the threads of thinking from the IB and apply them to children's experiences anywhere in the world. How can our school curriculum encourage children to understand that 'other people, with their differences, can also be right'? How can we ensure that our children have the conceptual architecture to link ideas across grand narratives? How can they be 'of service to the world'?[5]

Writing about the particular challenges of curriculum planning in international schools (while acknowledging that these are challenges for all schools), Simon Watson writes: 'Given that we aim to educate people for a shared humanity, a school curriculum will require elements beyond the usual siloed, subject-based requirements.'[6] He goes on to list an almost overwhelming set of things that need to be considered in order to save the world (or, perhaps more accurately, us) from ourselves. This pressure exists in national settings too, of course, but international schools have to balance the expectations and laws of a host nation with the demands of the curriculum, and balance all of this with the diversity within the school demographic itself. It's not straightforward.

....

4 R. Mweti, We Are Scientists, *Hatching Minds* (25 August 2018) [blog]. Available at: https://migratingbirdteaching.com/2018/08/25/we-are-scientists.

5 R. Berger, *Leaders of Their Own Learning: Transforming Schools Through Student-Engaged Assessment* (San Francisco, CA: Jossey-Bass, 2014), p. 216.

6 S. Watson, Aim High, Work Smart, Care Deeply, in R. Blatchford (ed.), *The Secondary Curriculum Leader's Handbook* (Woodbridge: John Catt Educational, 2019), pp. 53–60 at p. 55.

What the IB and initiatives like the Common Ground Collaborative (which emerged from the International School of Brussels)[7] manage to do is place this complexity into a framework that is simple and connected. The Common Ground Collaborative outlines three connecting themes – concept, competency and character – around which the curriculum is designed. How does our learning link and connect around concepts? How do we ensure that our students develop the knowledge and skills they need in order to be competent, and the character to have a positive impact on the world around them? When we think in this way, we develop critical, conceptual and creative thinking which is built on knowledge and wrapped in compassion. It might also be called wisdom.

However, being internationally minded is not the sole preserve of the international schools system. There is some great practice going on in schools in the UK and beyond that offer some inspiring models that could be taken up anywhere.

I invited English teacher Chris Waugh to write about the curriculum work he is doing in New Zealand. Here is what he had to say.

A case study from New Zealand

At the turn of the 21st century, New Zealand's educators turned their energy to the redevelopment of our national school curriculum.[8] What had come before was easily recognised as a facsimile of the English school curriculum, with all the colonial values that this entails.

What emerged was an upending of that traditional approach. First came the vision, stating the intention that the school system produces citizens who are 'confident, connected, actively involved, and lifelong learners'. The curriculum then set out the process by which every school, in consultation with its community, represented in particular by their community-elected boards of trustees should build its own curriculum – one that must embody such virtues as high expectations, the Treaty of Waitangi (New Zealand's foundational document), community engagement, inclusion, cultural diversity … the list goes on.

7   See https://commongroundcollaborative.org/our_story/learning-ecosystem/#1534771928673-923780f9-c8dd.

8   See http://nzcurriculum.tki.org.nz/The-New-Zealand-Curriculum#collapsible3.

Well before specific learning areas are outlined, a set of 'key competencies' are named. These determine the capabilities our citizens must develop in order to become lifelong learners and include 'relating to others', 'participating and contributing', 'managing self' and, importantly, 'thinking'.

The learning areas are defined along lines familiar to many in Western education systems, but even there, a strong attempt was made to distil each subject down to its fundamentals. As examples: English in the New Zealand curriculum is defined by two strands, making meaning and creating meaning. Maths is about number and logic. In the arts, students must develop technical expertise and develop their faculties in communicating and interpreting in their discipline.

Alongside this very open scheme for the education of generations of New Zealanders is embedded the principle of teaching as inquiry. Teachers are placed in the central role in curriculum development, and the classroom has become the core venue.

Seventeen years in and this project has developed a highly professionalised and empowered teaching profession, and has created a landscape within which my classroom has been able to thrive. A brief outline of the specifics of this will do a lot to explain what effect these curriculum changes have had on schools and learning.

At my school, Mount Aspiring College, choice underpins everything that we do in the English learning area.

Teachers devise their own programmes of learning in order to create an overarching progression, sometimes over many years, allowing them to pursue their own interests and exercise their expertise, and allowing for students to ally themselves with content or approaches for which they have affinity. Learning in our country is not simply defined by a singular knowledge construct, but rather as a means to the greater end of developing people as defined by our curriculum vision. Diversity and choice in the programme offer is one of the means by which we achieve this.

In our school, students of English choose their own teacher and their own programme of learning. They are empowered to select on the basis of their interests, aspirations and, dare I say it, tastes. This has led to the development of strongly interconnected programmes. Instead of being divided up according to a given assessment standard, they have a depth and breadth. Often defined by genre, the programmes situate a series of texts in their historical and social location, showing how they fit into the bigger picture of art, philosophy and society.

An example of this is the 'Newspeak' programme, which begins with a study of the common linguistic effects in satire over the last 200 years, followed by the reading of George Orwell's *Nineteen Eighty-Four*, then an investigation into the use of logical fallacies in rhetorical speech leads to the students writing and performing their own propaganda speeches. Films such as *The Lives of Others* and *Minority Report* are studied to further explore the genre of dystopia and its historical underpinnings, and eventually students embark on their own independent programme of reading, listening and viewing that leads to a final report which contains their conclusions about the stylistic features and thematic trends of dystopian fiction and how these reflect the linguistic effects of political satire and the society of the author. One student wrote with great eloquence about the lyrics of Radiohead's song '2 + 2 = 5' and the fact that its use of that quote from Orwell's novel is evidence that we do indeed now live in the dystopia that he described. The student posited that his art has now become our culture, and argued that dystopias over the last 100 years have invariably arisen from the anxieties of the time.

While this choice is afforded to the students, the teachers are expected to exercise their professional judgement fully in selecting the texts, approaches and skills that their students will develop each year. The only limit to text selection is that they must be in English or te reo Māori, and that some New Zealand literature should be represented.

To further shift the locus of control towards students and their families, we have embarked on a project that uses micro-credentials to allow students to collaborate with their teachers to determine when, and how, they should be assessed on their progress. We put them in charge of their attainment, offering them true agency in relation to their pathway through learning. The students identify for themselves what they must do to achieve in school and, if they wish, submit work for accreditation at any time. Their portfolio of achievements (which sits alongside their digital work portfolios) is available to them at all times, allowing them and their families to access detailed and reliable information about their progress at any time.

Students can attain credentials in five areas of learning, from the traditional knowledge and skills that have long characterised school assessment, to new areas like reasoning and even for developing a certain disposition like perseverance or altruism. A student who volunteers their time to act for the good of others can gain credentials for this that have parity with those they may unlock in the classroom. Credentials can be unlocked in any setting, and students do not have to depend on a teacher to create the context for assessment. They are standards based, and if the standards are met, and evidence provided, then the credential is awarded. While none of these ideas are in themselves radical, or even original, it takes a curriculum that prioritises the whole learner to create a foundation for this kind of innovation in school.

These mechanisms of choice, transparency and devolution of control are all supported by the vision of the New Zealand curriculum. I am proud to live in a country that is capable of articulating such a broad and optimistic vision for the outcome of its education system, and I am grateful that I am so highly valued as an educational professional.

Ours, at its best, is indeed a curriculum of hope.

What Chris outlines here is a model that is deeply rooted in community at a national level, but also at a school level – the choices students are allowed to make offer them a sense of agency and ownership, while there is still recognition of the expertise of the teacher in using those choices to select appropriate and sufficiently challenging texts for the students. This lends credibility to the process. Allowing students to 'choose' their teacher may seem controversial, but it demonstrates a deep trust in the professional capabilities of all the teachers in the team, while also recognising that students might be drawn to different styles of teaching or personality types (just as we are in life). Knowing that all your staff are capable and qualified and yet understanding that they might differ in their approach allows a leadership team to put faith in the staff they employ and allows students to exercise reasoned and responsible decision-making. It's a brave thing to do, but what Chris' school shows is that such trust can pay dividends.[9]

---

9   Examples of Chris' work in New Zealand can be found at: http://achieve.mtaspiring.edutronic.net (micro-credentials project); http://newspeak.edutronic.net (newspeak programme of learning); http://chris.edutronic.net/grammar-for-writing-dystopian-openings-outline (dystopian writing programme); http://mtaspiring.edutronic.net/year-12-course-selection-2 (example of Year 12 student choice); and http://bella.mtaspiring.edutronic.net (example of student blog).

Chapter 8

Tending to Saplings

A Curriculum of Hope in the Primary Classroom

It's not just stuff in our own brains. We can use it to help the world. This topic is really helpful because it's happening at this moment and we can act on it.

Year 5 child, St Ebbe's Church of England Aided Primary School, Oxford

One key aspect of the work I do in schools is to explore the difference between empathy and active compassion. Empathy is an emotional state, and if we're not careful we can overload children with an expectation that they will develop empathy in all kinds of contexts (often with a hidden agenda of compliance):

- There are children starving in Africa! (Eat your food.)

- There are people drowning in the Mediterranean! (Think yourself lucky to have a home.)

- The polar bears are dying! (Cut your electricity bill.)

On its own, empathy can lead to passivity or even compassion fatigue. It can impact on our mental health, making us feel powerless. Active compassion, on the other hand, is solution-focused and can be practised in ways that allow children to feel they have an element of control over situations that might otherwise feel hopeless. Empathy is a part of this, but in a way that moves us towards empowerment. It is an integral part of a pedagogy of power. In such ways the curriculum acts compassionately towards the child as well as encouraging the child to act compassionately towards others.

At the heart of this is perception. Placing children in situations in which their perception is pivoted in order to understand (to borrow from the IB again) that 'other people, with their differences, can also be right' requires some flexibility and skill. When done well, this can manifest itself powerfully in the way that children approach complex dilemmas.

Curriculum and community

At St Bernard's RC Primary in Ellesmere Port, the children work in partnership with Chester Zoo (community), utilising their knowledge of climate, continents, countries, animals and habitats to think about how they could protect Indonesian songbirds from extinction (credibility), linking to broader work on conservation across the whole network of schools in the teaching school alliance and the wider curriculum (coherence). The children create a protest within the local community to exhibit their knowledge and ideas for possible solutions in the form of artwork and song (creativity), in the hope of raising awareness and concern (compassion). Their approach is nuanced because by working in partnership with zoologists and conservationists, they have to consider the points of view of people in Indonesia and the wider economic and cultural factors impacting on the market for song-birds. One child explains:

> We don't want to be mean to them or be disrespectful to them because if you're just going up to them and saying 'you need to stop this!' you could be hurting their culture and we wouldn't like it if they said 'you can't have Christmas anymore or Halloween', so we need to be careful how we do it, like show them different ways to do it.
>
> Year 6 pupil, St Bernard's RC Primary, Ellesmere Port

The work at St Bernard's has now spread across the North West of England, involving 82 schools across Ellesmere Port, Chester and the Wirral, and the inter-relationship between the children, the zoo and the local community has been astounding. Working together in partnership, the children have:

- Raised thousands of pounds for wildlife conservation projects across the world.

- Planted hundreds of trees.

- Created wildlife meadows and animal sanctuaries.

- Persuaded eight local businesses to stop using single-use plastics.

- Persuaded parents to stop buying products containing non-sustainable palm oil.

- Worked with Chester Zoo, local politicians and businesses to make Chester the world's first Sustainable Palm Oil City.

- Created beautiful writing with real purpose to inform and campaign.

- Taken over Chester Zoo, undertaking the jobs of zoo rangers for the day and leading presentations for visitors.

- Written and recorded a song ('Let Our Voices Be Heard') that they intend to release as a single to raise money for wildlife projects.

- Passed their SATs.

Leading the project, Andy Moor, head of the Ignite Teaching School Alliance, says:

The real and urgent nature of the conservation challenge we face presents great opportunities for children to develop their own voice and to effect change. Conservation requires that they not only learn about issues, but that they take action themselves and effect change both locally and globally.

Developing a curriculum that enables young people to thrive and to meet the global conservation challenges facing our planet was the double challenge given to the school leaders participating in the IgniteZoo18 project. How can they design a meaningful curriculum for their school that embraces conservation challenges, whilst also challenging attitudes and reinvigorating pedagogical practice?

Sitting at the heart of the pedagogical process was the story and dilemma-led learning, and the children were taken through multiple points of view to understand the complexity of the issues before them. The kind of understanding demonstrated by the child quoted at the start of this chapter does not happen by accident. Working with me and Hywel Roberts, the staff learned how to introduce that hitherland knowledge into the learning process. Andy goes on to explain:

Using this approach, teachers stepped into the role of a palm oil plantation worker, a family who have lost their home through deforestation, an orangutan that has been separated from its family, and a wildlife trafficker. They created stories and challenges that the children were to navigate through. By layering essential knowledge into the process, different points of view could be considered in a most powerful way. We explored through the project the impact this had on learning, attitudes, pupil action and the development of empathy.

The way that curriculum has been constructed in this warm and collaborative network of schools has allowed children to genuinely make a difference to their local community and become a force for change. Working closely together, the schools have moved forward to add another shared unit of work to their collaboration: the 'Adrift' project, which is based around the difficulties faced by refugees, building another community link with a theatre company and with local refugee charities. The impact on the children is significant. As one 9-year-old said, 'We can change the world.'

Working alongside these schools and teachers over the past three years has been a wonderful process to witness. Hywel and I have taught in schools across the network with teachers watching, we have led INSETs and CPD, planned units of work and trained the education team at Chester Zoo. The schools recognised that curriculum alterations alone were not enough: pedagogy and assessment were integral elements of the work. They truly have created a curriculum of hope through a pedagogy of power.

....

A capacity to deal with complexity is something that is very much embedded in a curriculum of hope, as is the capacity to comfortably work within the realm of uncertainty. In a curriculum of hope, the ideas we are exploring are deliberately situated in the grey areas of human action and choice so that children are wading knee-deep in dilemma. It leads to this kind of feedback, offered by Peter Thonemann, professor of ancient history at Oxford University, after encountering some Year 3 pupils at St Ebbe's in Oxford who were exploring the cave paintings of the Stone Age:

For me, the most impressive aspect of the Year 3 Stone Age presentation was their ability to explain (very articulately) multiple interpretations of the cave art, without feeling the need to settle on one 'true' meaning. As two of the Year 3s explained to me, the 'lifestyle' scene in the cave (based on a real cave painting) shows a series of figures who might be in a procession or at a banquet, might be humans, might be gods, might be a single scene or might be three different scenes. The pupils were clearly quite content with the idea that we are just never going to know for certain, and can only make more or less plausible guesses.

I found this startling. I teach history and art history at university, and even very clever 18-year-old historians often find it difficult to live with epistemic uncertainty – the idea that we simply might not have the evidence to come down firmly in favour of one or another interpretation of an image or historical event. The ability to live comfortably with uncertainty in historical interpretation, and be content with the idea that the 'true' answer might always remain out of reach, is an extraordinarily high-level analytical skill in historical analysis, which many young people simply never get to at all. This is certainly not a skill that one necessarily gains through studying history at Key Stage 4 and Key Stage 5, in which 'uncertainty' is explicitly excluded from assessment criteria and methods! To see early Key Stage 2 pupils already having mastered it was truly amazing.

The children are comfortable with epistemic uncertainty because the dilemma is more important than being 'right'. The inherent interest of inquiry drives children to be happy to grapple with the unknown and to utilise what they know, are yet to know and will never know to best effect to understand and explain a problem.

When Tina Farr took over the headship at St Ebbe's, she already knew she wanted to redesign the curriculum – long before Ofsted made it a focus of the new framework for inspection. We had worked together at her old school, Carswell, to develop dilemma-led learning in classrooms. Staff and parents had been hugely impressed with the impact it had on learning, so she wanted to do this and more in her new role. At the heart of Tina's vision for her school was community – wanting the curriculum to involve the community as much as possible and to reach out to be of service to that community, so she set about building genuine partnership planning:

> In order to achieve this, we asked parents to join leaders and governors in holding an umbrella over our school to create the conditions in which creativity and risk-taking can flourish. We asked parents to hold us to account for educating wise, skilled, thoughtful citizens rather than just the things that can be easily measured. Their part in this is crucial.

Having set up a number of meetings with and presentations to governors and parents, the school started to move towards a shared vision for learning and for curriculum. By the time I went in to work with the teachers for a week, the governors were well on board and helping to shape this vision with the head. One of them created a curriculum vision document to help clarify the concepts being explored and two governors came to meet with me to talk through their ideas about curriculum and my intentions. It was a meeting of minds.

Working with each year group for a half day at a time, we began to construct overarching themes, all linked to narratives that would connect the curriculum, and then mapped on content and coverage to see where we might have gaps. What we found was that we were 'covering' far more than the national curriculum asked of us. Central to this process was the fact that both Tina and her deputy, Clare Whyles, sat in on each meeting so they would have an overview of a child's whole experience as they moved through the school curriculum. It also helped to build a sense of trust and collaboration between the teaching and leadership teams. Tina says:

> My deputy and I joining each planning session has meant that our teachers are safe in the knowledge that we are accountable too – we made these

decisions together. This also gave us an unprecedented insight into the skills and passions of our staff team. Using Dylan Wiliam's *Principled Curriculum Design*,[1] we came to understand that the real curriculum is not the national curriculum but what is created by teachers every day for their children, in their classrooms. Involvement of the senior leadership team at the planning stage seemed crucial for consistency and coherence.

As we worked, staff began to see that their concerns about, for example, getting enough writing from children, dissipated. Tina continues:

We found that writing just 'locked' on top of the rich content. We didn't need to plan for cross-curricular writing any more – it's just there, staring us in the face with a clarity of audience and purpose I haven't seen before.

Fast forward a few months and Year 3 are showing their parents, members of their local community and (as you have read) an Oxford don around their exhibition of Stone Age art; Year 4 are presenting at Oxford Council and hosting a climate change convention; and Year 5 are presenting the outcomes of their work around living in a world with fresh air. The school is alive with curiosity, questions, investigations and genuine deep learning.

Each year group's learning sits around unifying themes that connect all the units of work across the year, and which aim to build over time to a broader understanding of the world and human endeavour within it:

- Reception class: Beauty and wonder (appreciating our world).

- Year 1: Belonging and friendship (connecting with others).

- Year 2: The elements – earth, fire, air and water (understanding the world).

- Year 3: Human marks upon the world (the traces we leave on the world).

- Year 4: Human vs. nature (can we control our world?).

- Year 5: Power and leadership (how can we make the world a better place?).

---

1 D. Wiliam, *Redesigning Schooling – 3: Principled Curriculum Design* (London: Specialist Schools and Academies Trust, 2013). Available at https://webcontent.ssatuk.co.uk/wp-content/uploads/2013/09/Dylan-Wiliam-Principled-curriculum-design-chapter-1.pdf.

- Year 6: Exploration and invention (how do we know so much about our world and what more is there to discover?).

Each of these themes is broken down into individual units of inquiry with deep questions at their heart – for example:

- Who owns a country? (borders and migration)
- How could we feed 10 billion people? (food, populations and sustainability)
- How can we help other people feel like they belong? (intergenerational project with the local community)
- What clues does the Earth leave us to tell us the story of its history? (evolution and geology)

Onto these is mapped the content of the national curriculum and more, but beneath that is a process steeped in story and possibility – our 'Let's say …' scenarios. Story is the beating heart of the curriculum.

Some of the planning documents for St Ebbe's can be found in the appendix: The Seed Catalogue.

I've inherited an old QCA scheme of work. No one who qualified post-2005 in England will have the faintest idea what I'm talking about, but suffice to say that if anyone reading this still teaches the Great Fire of London, it's because it once appeared on some exemplar materials for the national curriculum and has remained stubbornly present ever since. How many of our schemes and units of work are born out of habit from long ago?

Anyway, Great Fire it is. We're in Yorkshire, about 200 miles and 350 years away from this event, and so my first challenge is to help the children 'connect' to this time and place. They have read a short information text for homework, rather than leading their parents down the path towards divorce by having to make a Tudor house that we're planning to burn down later. A short reading task with a little research built in – easy to do and they can still go out for a family trip to the park. All is good.

On Monday morning they come into school and I engage the concept of 'novelty' to get their attention. Cognitive science is now catching up with teachers on acknowledging the role of curiosity in motivation and learning, but many of us already knew.[2] On this day, I'm engaging their curiosity by taking them to the hall where there is a sign stating that 'Authorised Personnel Only' are permitted to enter. We work out what this means. The children are told that they will know if they are authorised if the thumbprint software beeps when they put their thumbs on the piece of tinfoil I've attached to the door. They frown at me. I wink and nod. They smile. They put their thumbs on the tinfoil. I very obviously say 'beep' and they go in. Complicit in play.

I've got their attention and piqued their curiosity. They're not learning anything yet, but when I introduce the problem they're ready.

'Let's say we're on a building site in London – does anyone know anything about London? (Collecting prior knowledge which in this instance is scant.)

'OK, so yes, London is a big city – the capital city of England – kind of like the "boss" city where the government is … yes, and the queen … yes, that's right, Wembley Stadium.

'I'm going to speak to you now as a builder in this capital city of London. He has a problem and wants to tell you about it – he's hoping you might be able to help.' (Making them feel important – engaging emotion.)

I speak as the builder. No costume, no accent – there's no need. I simply say the words: 'My important work here has been stopped and I'm worried that I might not get my flats built. Last week my diggers were digging up the ground to lay foundations for these new homes for people who don't have a home at the moment, and they dug up these objects. Now I've been told I can't proceed – I can't carry on building – until we know if they are significant or important. (Note the emphasis on developing vocabulary.)

'I wondered if you might take a look at them for me and let me know whether you think they are significant – it looks like a lot of burned junk to me!'

....

2 S. Wade and C. Kidd, The Role of Prior Knowledge and Curiosity in Learning, *Psychonomic Bulletin and Review* 26(4) (2019): 1377–1387.

On the floor are several objects that I had set fire to with a blowtorch on Sunday afternoon. That's my kind of planning. There is a fragment of a diary extract with a date – 2 September 1666, a burned wooden baby rattle, a scorched leather satchel buckle and charred fragment of clothing. The children gather around the objects in groups and discuss.

When they feed back to me they tell me that they think the objects belong to a family fleeing from a fire – the Great Fire of London. They have read about it in their homework.

I act surprised. Teacher in role allows for all kinds of levels of ignorance to be displayed to children who then feel compelled to educate. It's just a tool for retrieval practice.

'Where did they go?' I ask

'We don't know!' they reply.

'I wonder …'

So we get out a map of London from that time and the children point to the river – there. Water. They go there.

There are some beautiful images of London burning painted from the perspective of people standing at the edge of the Thames. Some of the most powerful are by anonymous artists and are housed by the Society of Antiquaries in London. We have a look at some of them and discuss what it might have been like to be standing there. The sounds, the smells, the heat on your skin, the effect of the smoke on your eyes, on breathing …

The children create small family groups in still images, and I ask one child to help me with a problem.

'You're a boatman and you can take people across the river to safety.'

He nods eagerly.

'You have space for four people – how many trips are you going to have to make if there are 28 people to save?'

He works it out – he is a child who was celebrating when he entered the room because we weren't 'doing maths', but he is doing maths now. There are more calculations: the fire is 40 minutes away. It takes him 20 minutes to get there and back … It's not a maths lesson – just retrieval practice.

Over the course of the unit of work we meet many people affected by fire – like Hannah, the baker's daughter, scarred from the fire. We meet historians who disagree – some who think the fire may have killed more people than is officially recorded, some who think the fire brought an early end to the plague and some who don't. We consider the beneficial outcomes of the fire: better building regulations, a fire service, rubbish disposal so reduced risk of disease, beautiful new buildings. And we discuss the downsides: loss of life, home and livelihood, the plight of refugees, the inaction of the king, the long-term consequences for the refugees and the potentially thousands of people whose deaths went unrecorded. At the end of all this learning I ask the children to gather around me and I light a candle.

'Let's say we're back in the bakery on the night of 2 September 1666. The family are asleep upstairs. Mary, the maid, is sleeping in the next room. The fire has started but it's small. We can blow it out. Should we?'

The children look at me and each other and they start to talk. They discuss all the things that won't happen if we blow the candle out. Or might happen – later. They discuss the plague, the king and the new buildings that will emerge out of the ashes. They discuss the dead. And one child says, 'We can't play god. We have the chance to save at least six lives. We have to blow it out.'

So they do, but in doing so, they know they are living with uncertainty – epistemic uncertainty, I now know to say.

Curriculum and coherence

Fast forward ten years or so to Thorp Primary School in Oldham.

I'm planning a unit of work for Year 2 with head teacher Jenny Bowers. Jenny is passionate that the curriculum connects to the lived experiences of children and to the local community, so we are both scratching our heads and wondering why the Great Fire of London is still there, persistently smouldering like a stubborn curriculum ember. It's one of the units of work people seem to still like teaching – more than habit, there is a genuine attachment. And, of course, it appeared as 'suggested content' in the national curriculum as an example, so everyone thinks it's the law. There are other reasons though. 'We can link it to fire safety and we get the fire brigade in – the children love it!' is just one of the responses from teachers I've asked.

We have already decided on an overarching theme for the year group to create what Clare Sealy describes as horizontal links[3] across the year. These form concepts on which inquiry questions will be hung. Concepts allow us to choose a lens through which to explore a topic or subject. In turn these can then generate inquiry questions that help us to hone our focus so that children can practise their capacities to develop hypotheses, utilise knowledge and draw conclusions.

- Early Years Foundation Stage (EYFS): Who am I, and where did I come from? (me)

- Year 1: How do I connect to others in the world? (others)

- Year 2: How do human beings cope with change? (change)

- Year 3: How has humankind left its mark on the world? (inheritance)

- Year 4: How has humankind developed and relied on communication to thrive and survive? (communication)

- Year 5: Is man born to seek adventure? (endeavour)

- Year 6: Does man really have dominion over the Earth? (responsibility)

....

3   Sealy, The 3D Curriculum That Promotes Remembering.

One strand of the Year 2 question is the concept of 'the past', which generates a secondary subset of questions:

- What can I learn from those who went before me?

- How might the Fire of London have affected how we deal with fire today?

- What else was happening in 1666 that we might learn from?

- Do disasters affect rich and poor people differently, and why?

We suddenly find ourselves thinking about Eyam, the 'plague village', and before we know it we are extending a unit on the Great Fire of London into one on fire and pestilence. Two communities; two leaders; two disasters; one time. Concepts of sacrifice, civic duty and how they might link to religion and culture.

These are conceptual echoes that we can pick up on throughout the curriculum. When we look at pollution we can return to the notion of sacrifice for the common good in an action as simple as leaving the car at home and walking to school. We can think about keeping ourselves healthy and safe, echoing back to fire safety and hygiene when we consider, in another unit, the impact of flood waters on the population of Bangladesh. The differences between urban and rural which were explored through London and Eyam are picked up again in a future unit on evacuees, and in another on changes to our local area.

In addition, there is an echo around London itself. In one unit we see London ravaged by fire; in another by the Blitz; in another we see life in London through the eyes of a Victorian child labourer. In each of these there is an opportunity to compare life in this large city to life in a rural community – Eyam or the villages taking in child evacuees, or, more locally, the impact of the Industrial Revolution on children living in rural hamlets like Thorp during the Victorian period. The idea of 'where I have come from' is much more universally understood than simply creating a family tree (although that might happen too).

At two points within the year, the whole school comes together under a unifying theme that links all the year groups. For Armistice Day, there is a whole-school exploration of the Second World War, but with themes for each year group that link to the concepts and inquiries for their year groups:

- EYFS: What is peace? (helping characters in stories in conflict to make peace)

- Year 1: What was the role of medicine in the Second World War? (following on from their science work on hygiene and historical exploration of Florence Nightingale)

- Year 2: How did London take care of its children during the Blitz? (following on from the Great Fire of London – exploring the city in two different time periods)

- Year 3: How do we remember the war? (the things humankind does to mark its memories on the world)

- Year 4: How did animals help us to communicate during the war? (linking to the theme of communication across the year)

- Year 5: How did courageous individuals help us to win the war? (linking to the theme of endeavour for the year)

- Year 6: How can we make sure that war never happens again? (exploring causes and responsibilities that enable us to learn lessons from those causes – linking to the year's theme of responsibility)

Another touchpoint is Christmas. After some discussion, we decided that rather than cram Christmas in around other learning (which inevitably gets lost) we would embrace it. The whole-school unit on Christmas consists of:

- EYFS: Celebrations across religions – why do we give presents? (How does Christmas affect me?)

- Year 1: The Christmas story – from the point of view of Mary and Joseph – performed to parents with Year 2 (the others who shaped the story of Christmas).

- Year 2: The Christmas story – from the point of view of the innkeeper, shepherds and kings – history shaped by witnesses (how did Christmas change the lives of others?).

- Year 3: What are Christmas traditions – is it possible to keep them while being environmentally responsible? (inheritance)

- Year 4: How did the Christmas story spread across the world? (communication)

- Year 5: (continuing their Second World War focus) How did the war impact on Christmas? (endeavour)

- Year 6: Has the Christmas story got lost? – the power of consumerism and Christmas for the homeless (responsibility).

Each year group will contribute to a final presentation to parents. Years 1 and 2 will perform the Christmas story, but all aspects of the work will be shared through readings, songs and poetry created by the children.

Again, the work in this school is in its early stages, but the key concepts are helping to create lenses that allow the teachers to carefully select texts, materials and resources to allow for deeper conceptual understanding to emerge as the children move through school.

Creative curriculum: Mantle of the Expert and building communities of inquiry

Many of the classroom stories threaded throughout this book sit within a pedagogical framework of Mantle of the Expert. Conceived by Dorothy Heathcote[4] and developed by Luke Abbott and Tim Taylor,[5] Mantle of the Expert offers children the opportunity to practise responsibility by taking on the roles of a responsible team fulfilling the obligations of a commission from a fictional client. It is interesting that the Batman effect (see Chapter 3) is so named because of the impact of adopting a cloak. In Mantle of the Expert, the mantle is one of responsibility in which a child might adopt an attitude of adult responsibility towards the task given to them. It has, as you will see in the examples in this book, a powerful impact on children's language, investment and persistence.

Only a few years ago, some educationalists were deriding Mantle of the Expert as an example of poor practice, suggesting that it was not possible for children to be

....

4 D. Heathcote and G. Bolton, *Drama for Learning: Dorothy Heathcote's Mantle of the Expert Approach to Education* (London: Heinemann, 1995).

5 T. Taylor, *A Beginner's Guide to Mantle of the Expert: A Transformative Approach to Education* (Norwich: Singular Publishing, 2017).

'experts' because they are novices in learning.[6] In the six years since that claim was made, we have seen more evidence emerging about the power of narrative, the impact of using high-level vocabulary with children and the effect of role play on the ability to focus. However, like any pedagogy it can only be as good as the reality in practice. Tim Taylor's excellent book and website offer many examples of how this kind of planning can be deeply knowledgeable and meaningful for children.[7]

One of the key tenets of the work is the 'element of grace' – Heathcote's phrase to describe the complexity of human action and emotion. While tension and narrative drive the work, there is an underlying kindness resting on the assumption that while humankind might do bad things, there are often complex motivations and influences at work. Mantle of the Expert doesn't deal with villains and heroes; it deals with human beings in a mess and human beings endeavouring to solve problems.

At Woodrow First School in Redditch, the children encounter much (but not all) of their curriculum through Mantle of the Expert. Maths, phonics and other aspects of literacy are taught discretely, as is PE, but so much of the curriculum can be plaited into this way of working. During one visit I see children in Reception class engrossed in helping a farmer to work out who is eating his vegetables and crops; in another a community of monks are dealing with challenges from local businesses; in another staff from a scrapyard are helping the Iron Man. There is business and purpose everywhere. I asked head teacher Richard Kieran to write a short piece about why his school has found Mantle of the Expert so compelling.

Since 2010, Mantle of the Expert has been at the heart of our school curriculum. The school staff were at a point where they wanted more from the curriculum for our children. Mantle offered much that could be built upon: it has become the central tenet of the work we do. The unwritten mantra for the school, 'What more can we do for our children?' is embedded in all we do – for staff as well as children. Woodrow is fortunate in that our staff turnover is minimal – people stay because they want to teach with Mantle; they get that almost intangible oomph when they witness what children experience with this approach: tales, tensions and tasks.

6   D. Christodoulou, *Seven Myths About Education* (Abingdon and New York: Routledge, 2013).
7   See www.mantleoftheexpert.com.

The question we always ask is, 'What will interest the children and, indeed, the adults (although not necessarily engage or motivate)'? We look for an angle that fascinates children. The planning process becomes a whole school doing – advice is shared readily and one year group will support another. Spontaneous seminars and mini tutorials can be seen as we ask what could, might or will work.

Staff are free to choose training opportunities and courses whenever they think it will make a difference. The school also works closely and shares an annual training day with a partner school in Newcastle – because it is good to talk, challenge, question and compare. We are an underground multi-academy trust.

Wandering around Woodrow gives a better picture of the school. Displays are not wallpaper or window dressing; they tell the story of what is happening in each class – meeting times, lists, images, plans, maps, photos, biographies of the client, weather forecasts, transport, action plans – all constructed by the children with their teachers, not unlike props for a theatre production. The nub of this is to provoke the staff and children. A provocative approach can do so much to stimulate thinking, writing, a point of view, tension – it goes way beyond and so much deeper than engagement and wow. There are no stickers, learning objectives or zone boards. High demand and high expectation are inseparable partners.

The children will tell you they are happy stepping in and out of role. It doesn't require any grand gestures from their teachers or each other. Just a subtle change of language to the inductive. Moments of silence are not necessarily there to be filled with the awkward – rather they are seen as spaces where thoughts can flourish.

Relationships in the school are key to its strength. It is important to get on and be nice. Teachers will be more motivated in an atmosphere that pro-motes support and encouragement, and children will be more confident to explore the curriculum in a space that is safe.

So Mantle is at the heart of our curriculum because:

- Children make decisions about how to do something, and through discus-sion and distributed leadership these are woven into the learning by the teacher. Because of this there is a sense of agency and motivation to learn. Relationships between teacher and children are strong when working in this way. Children are able to talk about Mantle and their learning confidently and articulately to visitors.

- The drama-based method is a sequence of highly planned, active classroom tasks that lead learners into an imaginary, emotional and intellectual relationship with the curriculum. This approach offers the children power to influence learning and the class 'buy in' to the curriculum which leads to deep learning experiences.

- Mantle is concerned with short-term cognitive gains and acquisition of knowledge within longer term educational goals. The contexts explored lead to genuine conversations about real-life situations; beliefs are shared and explored as well as respected. The responsible team in Mantle is concerned with the values of care and respect. They learn to deal with cause and consequence; tension and justice. The intended outcomes play their part in developing personal fulfilment and well-being. They begin to contribute to social justice and inclusion.

- Teachers constantly reflect, assess and adapt when teaching with Mantle; this enables high expectations to be the norm. Language and dialogue is central to the work as the client, or the team, or the tension demands more of the children. Whilst Mantle frames the children as experts, teachers are vigilant in their assessment of knowledge in order to address any misconceptions which may become evident.

- The careful structuring of tasks moves children along a continuum in Mantle from attraction to productive obsession. Intellectual, social and emotional support provides scaffolds for learning. The work is linked to research by Minchi Kim and Michael Hannafin[8] and Sadhana Puntambekar and Janet Kolodner[9] – namely solving problems. Tasks are deliberate and inquiry based: problem identification, exploration, reconstruction, presentation and communication, reflection and negotiation.

- Mantle requires teachers to draw on a range of strategies when teaching using this approach. Whole-class, structured group work, guided learning and individual activity are all integral to this way of learning. The class is

---

8 M. C. Kim and M. J. Hannafin, Scaffolding 6th Graders' Problem-Solving in Technology-Enhanced Science Classrooms: A Qualitative Case Study, *Instructional Science: An International Journal of the Learning Sciences* 39(3) (2011): 255–282.

9 S. Puntambekar and J. L. Kolodner, Toward Implementing Distributed Scaffolding: Helping Students Learn Science from Design, *Journal of Research in Science Teaching* 42(2) (2005): 185–217.

constantly moving in and out of the fictive context which they are creating in order to learn the knowledge and skills necessary to complete a task. The fiction creates a purpose for curriculum learning.

- As a dramatic inquiry-based approach, learning in Mantle is driven by a series of inquiry questions. Mantle uses a combination of higher and lower order questions to generate successful learning. Mantle is dialogic – it harnesses the power of talk to stimulate and extend children's thinking.

- Mantle is an approach which provides rich learning opportunities for all learners. As described by Susan Hart and colleagues,[10] we are a community of learners with the principles of co-agency, trust and everybody at the core. Teacher and learner share responsibility for learning without a predetermined limit on ability. Opportunities for learning are planned which will be part of a shared experience where everyone is important.

Many of the lessons and inquiries I describe throughout this book could easily be taught through Mantle of the Expert. The idea that a responsible team is solving a problem for a person in a place with a problem is a powerful vehicle for learning.

Curriculum with compassion

Julie Rees, the head teacher at Ledbury Primary School in Herefordshire, has always placed values at the heart of the child's experience. Walk into her school and you are enveloped in warmth and joyfulness. The grounds of the school are teeming with children learning outdoors; classrooms are calm as children use peer massage and mindfulness to help each other to focus and settle. Bailey, the school dog, is a well-loved member of the school family. But everyone wanted a little bit more from the curriculum itself and wanted that curriculum to match the values around compassion embedded in the culture of the school.

To build more coherence into the history elements of the curriculum, we decided to work in a backwards chronological way. It made no sense to us that Key Stage

10 S. Hart, A. Dixon, M. J. Drummond and D. McIntyre, *Learning without Limits* (Maidenhead: Open University Press, 2004).

1 looked at random events and people with no sense of how they connected in time, and then that Key Stage 2 began tens of thousands of years ago and accelerated quickly towards the Victorians at breakneck speed. We changed things around a little:

- Reception: The here and now – 'in my lifetime'.
- Year 1: Living memory – 'in my family's lifetimes'.
- Year 2: Victorian times.
- Year 3: Tudor times (in Ledbury you can't really avoid the Tudors).
- Year 4: Normans, Vikings and Anglo-Saxons.
- Year 5: Ancient civilisations – Romans, Egyptians and Greeks.
- Year 6: Very ancient civilisations – Stone Age (linking to evolution and fossils).

That chronological decision helped us to map other elements of the curriculum too. If you're going to look at early humankind, there is an obvious link to evolution. The Victorians lend themselves to explorations and discoveries in science, and the Tudors to explorations and discoveries of the wider world.

We then, as with the other schools explored in this chapter, decided on themes that would link across year groups, although the year would be structured into three blocks for all groups:

1. Autumn: Learning from the past.
2. Spring: Being in the present.
3. Summer: Looking to the future.

For example, Year 2 might look like this:

Rights and responsibilities		
Children's rights	Animal rights	Our responsibilities
Learning from the past (Victorians)	Being in the present (The zoo)	Looking to the future (Improving our local community)

Within each of these elements is a world of knowledge. For example, in their zoo project the children have to consider the idea that there is to be a new worldwide treaty on the rights of animals, which has embedded into it the expectation that, in future, zoos will only keep collections of animals in the biome or climate zone in which they occur naturally. What kind of knowledge would the children need in order to relocate animals if that were the agreement?

They also have to evaluate the pros and cons of such a decision, whether it is practical or desirable and whether other measures might be more beneficial. They might have to talk to an expert, find out what zoos currently do to protect animals for climate differences and whether zoos themselves have an opinion on the matter.

They may also have to consider why it might be that we could one day have animals that no longer fit into any zoo because their natural climate and habitat have disappeared. What would we do with them?

It's solution-focused thinking, it's playful and imaginative, but it's also deeply rooted in real-life problems and possibilities.

As we explore the pedagogy that might underpin the curriculum, I model a lesson for Year 5 to show how people, place, problem and possibility could spark off a unit of work on our responsibilities to our planet.

....

Let's say … Year 5 are sitting on the carpet looking up politely at the stranger in their classroom who has turned up to teach them today. They don't usually sit on the carpet – that's for infants, isn't it? But I want them close to me and to be able to get up and down without having to navigate furniture. You have to be nimble when you're going to Mars, but they don't know that yet.

'Let's say we're in a bedroom. It belongs to a young woman. Not very young – she's old enough to have been to university and to have built up a successful career. How old might that be? What might be a good name for her?'

The children suggest Mary, 32 years old. So Mary it is.

'She's back in her childhood bedroom – it's not changed much even though she's lived in her own place for a while now. Her parents have kept all her old things in here. There are photos and medals and certificates and reminders of her childhood – perhaps you can work with a partner and show me what we might find in this room?'

We build up a picture of Mary's character – from horse-riding rosettes to teddy bears, from 'star of the week' certificates to photographs of her old dog. With every contribution the children's investment in Mary grows, so she begins to matter to them.

I sit at a small desk with a piece of paper in front of me. I'm holding a pen.

'Let's say Mary is sitting in this childhood room of hers and writing a letter. I'll read a little of it and we can think about what might be happening and why she's here.

Dear Mum and Dad,

By the time you read this, I'll be gone. I never was any good at goodbyes, was I? Remember the time you dropped me off at university and I walked away without even looking back? You were so cross at the time. I wasn't being cruel – I just didn't want you to see me cry. I don't want you to see me cry now. But this is the hardest goodbye of all, knowing I'll never see you again.

'Oh. What do we think might be happening here?'

The children are quick to offer suggestions – they think she might be dying. One thinks she might be moving to Australia. Another thinks she might be going to war.

'I'll read some more – maybe there's more information about what she's doing.

I know you don't understand, but this is something I have to do. I've worked so hard for this and the future of the human species is at stake …

'Oh. There's a date at the top of the letter too – I'll write it on the board. 2030. I wonder what she means – can anyone come up with a plausible theory about what might be happening. What's a plausible theory?' And we're off …

The children offer lots of theories and generate questions. I prompt them, 'What do we need to know? If you can ask her a question, what would the most important question be?'

They hot-seat me as Mary under the condition that she will only answer five questions, so they need to make them count. By the time they have asked four, they are still no closer to understanding where she is going. Time is running out.

'You have one question left – what do we need to find out?'

'Mary, where are you going?'

'I'm going to Mars.'

There is an audible gasp from the children. Part delight, part excitement, part surprise. The child with autistic spectrum disorder who has been sitting with his teaching assistant slips out from behind his desk and comes to join the class on the carpet. It turns out that he knows a lot about space and there is no way he is missing out on this.

'If she's going to Mars and says she won't see her parents again, does that suggest she might not be coming back? Why?'

The children speculate that perhaps it takes so long to get there that there will be no time to return. We create a physical number line to estimate how long the journey might take. Their guesses run from one to 20 years. I drop in a fact: when Mars and the Earth are closest together it could take as little as seven months to get there, so why might she not come back? A child speaks up. He is normally quiet but not today.

'Fuel. They might not have enough fuel to get back.'

'Why don't they take spare fuel?'

'It might make the spacecraft too heavy and create damaging G-force.'

I write G-force on the board. I'd not anticipated this. I'm going to have to brush up on my knowledge of G-force.

'What other problems might we face that might mean we don't come home?'

There is a little ripple of excitement as the word 'we' lands in their hearts. They scribble ideas down on sticky notes and we make a list:

- G-force.
- Gravity.
- Atmosphere.
- Temperature.
- Food supplies.
- Biodiversity.
- No pollinators.
- Strange bacteria and viruses (we might not have immunity).
- Keeping our sanity.
- Lack of oxygen.
- Storms (this later develops into a concern about solar radiation).
- Lack of water.
- Lack of plants.
- Energy.
- An accident.

They are not fully aware of it but they have written their own curriculum, and I'm getting a genuine sense of what they already know and what their misconceptions are. For example, while they have deduced that it will be much colder on Mars because it is further away from the sun, some have assumed that there will be ice on Mars. Some have pointed out that there is a 'thin' atmosphere on Mars and too little oxygen, but they don't realise that our own atmosphere has more nitrogen in it than oxygen, so we look at the chemical composition of the atmospheres of both planets.

'We're going to need a lot of trees!' shouts out one when they find out how much CO_2 is in the Martian atmosphere.

Working out possible solutions to these problems will take some time, and along the way there will be some very traditional teaching – probably in the form of a lecture for the young astronauts, probably at NASA, probably by their teacher in role as Mary …

But as we move forward, I know that there is a lot of existing knowledge in the room. Every child knew that trees take in CO_2 and give out oxygen. Most understood the concept of gravity and its relation to mass. As soon as they saw that Mars had 38% of the gravitational force of Earth, they were talking about the impact on their bodies, their muscles, their weight – after all, they are the Tim Peake and Brian Cox generation. We can build on that knowledge. Test it. We can read information texts about the projects NASA are running to create plants that might survive (under cover) on Mars. We can explore all the science and more because they gave me more than I might have anticipated.

One of the items on their list intrigues me: 'Keeping our sanity? What do you mean?'

'People could go mad with loneliness up there … And they won't have phones or gadgets – there's no infrastructure – no masts or satellites pointing the right way … And if food runs short, they could turn on each other – maybe even start eating each other!'

Such a contribution would be impressive from any child, but from a child who began the lesson snuggled up to his teaching assistant, away from the other children because of his autism, it's a lump in the throat contribution.

'How might we keep our sanity then?'

'Take books?'

'Which would be the best books to take? The best books ever written?'

We have a lot of work to do. A lot to learn. Dozens of problems to solve. It is daunting but they are up for the challenge. And they don't yet know what the main challenge is going to be. It is looming on the horizon. A protest outside their headquarters. It turns out there is a twist in the pathway ahead: 'What gives you the right to go to another planet when you've taken so little care of this one?'

But that's in the future … another unit. A sequence, you might say.

This approach of building on prior knowledge, of allowing scope for unplanned knowledge to be wrapped into the process, and of leaving space for new ideas, connections and solutions to be co-constructed makes the learning matter to the children. You can see here how this lesson evolved into the 'A Mission to Mars' unit of work in the pupil referral unit in Chapter 5, although engineered to suit their particular context. Whether they are Key Stage 2 in a mainstream setting or Key Stage 3 in alternative provision, the context is equally compelling. It appeals to the human sense of adventure.

When I met the wonderful Dorothy Heathcote all those years ago, the seemingly simple advice she gave me was the best guidance I've ever had: 'Start where the children are at, not where you think they might or should be.' What they already know is valued; what they need to know is negotiated; the reason they need to know is present, exciting and wrapped in a story. It is clear with this example that a great deal of time might have been wasted had I assumed the children knew nothing.

This model of learning, and those elsewhere in this chapter, are a million miles away from Ofsted's tabula rasa approach. It leans more towards the vision of the Welsh government or the IB, but, nevertheless, it is perfectly possible to work in this way whatever national model we find ourselves working within.

Chapter 9

Cultivating Hope
(in Trying Times)

When we move forward in our own schools, making decisions that best fit our context, we can sometimes feel overwhelmed by the conflicting demands of choice and constraint. Where will we find the time to write curriculum? We won't unless we lose something else. No school team can add this to an existing workload, so we need to work out what we can shed – what David Cameron (the educationalist, not the former prime minister) calls 'the breakable plates'.[1] We can identify those plates precisely because they *are* breakable – losing them won't impact directly on the quality of the children's experience. They may impact on the amount of evidence gathering and surveillance-based systems that have become habitual in some schools, but all the stories in this book have been characterised by trust and collegiality – schools working together with a shared sense of purpose. This means that teachers need to be trusted to try new ways of working; space needs to be made by senior leaders for them to develop subject knowledge, think carefully about how their curriculum coheres and what the experience of the child will be. Teachers need to be able to take risks and to have the capacity to manage those risks.

Hope lies in trust.

Much of the work described in this book is rooted in a sense of agency – there is a process of co-construction of curriculum experience with children. Whether that manifests itself in the kind of direct choice offered by Chris Waugh's school in New Zealand, in the generation of lists of problems and possibilities by the Year 5 class in Ledbury or in the direct actions of pupils in Chester, the children are empowered to have a sense of ownership of their learning, and this ownership

1 D. Cameron, Raising Attainment, Being Creative … and Surviving. Speech delivered at the University of Chichester Academy Trust conference, 5 September 2016.

heightens their sense of responsibility and purpose. This also requires that we relinquish some of the structures and scaffolds which have perhaps led to dependency in the system – dependency not only by children, but also by teachers. Moving towards independence requires a sense of empowerment.

Hope lies in agency.

Deep questions drive interest and investment in a curriculum of hope. Within these pages, we have seen many forms of inquiry emerging. This is not the spectral mode of inquiry that some confuse with teachers relinquishing all responsibility and control in a classroom. That is just poor practice. This kind of inquiry-led learning is driven by big questions that are not easily answered and which generate more questions. In such a curriculum there is no 'end', only more possibility for exploration. The curriculum ignites curiosity so the children want to take their learning forward into adult life. This can only happen if they are led by a curious adult who sees their job as not limited to being the transmitter of all they already know, but also a learner in their own right.

Hope lies in curiosity.

Relationships are vital to this way of working. Teachers and children are taking risks together – adopting roles can be deeply exposing for both parties. This aspect of vulnerability requires teachers to play, experiment and demonstrate not only the extent and limitations of their own knowledge, but also to have the agility to adapt to the unexpected. It is not easy or simple, but it is deeply powerful and memorable. That vulnerability extends to senior leaders who need to act as an umbrella to protect staff and children from the pressures exerted on schools, but who also need to be able to acknowledge how those pressures can influence their own behaviours and well-being. Being open and communicative about these impacts can create a school environment where people feel they can pull together to work in the children's best interests.

Hope lies in vulnerability.

As teachers, children, leaders, parents and other stakeholders work together to build curriculum that reaches out to the community, and allows the community to reach in, the curriculum extends beyond the walls of the school – beyond the walls of subject and beyond the walls of labels towards a mutual understanding. If we are to move children beyond a notion of social mobility (where in effect they are taught to want to leave their communities behind) towards a model of social growth (in which they work to improve and support their communities), we see curriculum moving towards a common good.

Hope lies in community.

All of this is done in a spirit of play, particularly iterative and purposeful play, in which shared endeavour is what Mary Myatt describes as 'high challenge, low threat'.[2] The playfulness encourages laughter, it creates safe spaces in which mistakes can be made and learned from, and it provides a buffer for children from what can be big problems in the world. This interaction and interdependence between responsibility and play makes for safe, secure but stimulating learning in which children can practise adulthood without losing a sense of being a child.

Hope lies in play.

Hope is resilient, persistent and finds a way.

---

2   M. Myatt, *High Challenge, Low Threat: How the Best Leaders Find the Balance* (Woodbridge: John Catt Educational, 2016).

Appendix

The Seed Catalogue
– Some Examples
of Planning

In this appendix I share some of the approaches to planning taken by schools with whom I have been working. They are outlines, not detailed lesson-by-lesson planning, but hopefully they will provide some inspiration.

When we have come together to reshape the curriculum in primary schools, we have done so largely by following this process:

1. Let's look at units of work we already cover that we think we do well and love to teach. Write all that down.

    (We love teaching the Great Fire of London and evacuees in Year 2.)

2. What do those things have in common? Where are the links and connections that might help us to focus on a particular concept across a year group?

    (London is a link – as is surviving disaster – perhaps resilience could be a concept?)

3. How can that concept guide some inquiry questions linked to the content we know we want to keep intact?

    (How do human beings overcome adversity?)

    What other units of work might fit well with that question to broaden out the curriculum?

    (We usually do plants and animal habitats – we could explore a question such as, 'How can human beings help plants and animals to overcome adversity?')

4. Where should we start (the people/place/problem/possibilities of the story that will allow us to step into the content and to build a contextual frame)?

(People: a refugee from the fire. Place: a field outside London. Problem: she has nowhere to live. Possibilities: who got their homes rebuilt and why? What happened to the people who didn't get their homes rebuilt? Does the fire tell us a story about how differently people were treated at this time in history? If we were to help her, what could we do and what would we need to know?)

5. How can this story guide us so that curriculum objectives are plaited or pulled in – for example, could we map the place or consider where this moment sits on a timeline?

6. What elements of other subject areas can be taught either as part of the natural flow of this narrative or can be retrieved and practised in a context? For example, what is the area of this room? How many rooms will we need? What percentage of people will be left over?

7. Where are the opportunities for talk, writing and reading?

8. How do we layer on vocabulary so the children are learning rich new words as they go along? Can role be utilised to encourage them to reach for an adult/professional language register?

9. How does this unit link to that unit?

10. How does this year fit with that year? What is the story of our curriculum?

In a typical secondary setting, mapping needs to be done on two levels: within subject areas (which could be planned as above) and across subject areas, finding common links wherever possible. This requires whole-school mapping of curriculum at a senior leader level, as well as heads of department having access to other subjects' long-term plans. Departments can't make meaningful links unless they have the whole picture, and they can't process the whole picture unless they have time to coordinate and cooperate with other middle leaders.

Too often, middle leader meeting time is spent on information-giving rather than in getting together to talk about curriculum. However, these discussions can be very fruitful, as the English/science/maths example from Haiti shows (in Chapter 4). Even something as simple as a teacher of one subject saying to students, 'I know you're studying X in this subject and we're doing Y because they connect,' can be hugely powerful. The following pages offer some examples of how these connections are forming in other schools.

Wales

The plaits offered here represent our thoughts as we initially mapped out our lines of inquiry, linking the subjects of the area of learning and experience together. These are examples of how we might represent the overview of a unit of work. There is also an overview of how the team fleshed out their unit on *The Explorer* in a medium-term plan and a medium-term overview of the *Sea Empress* local study.

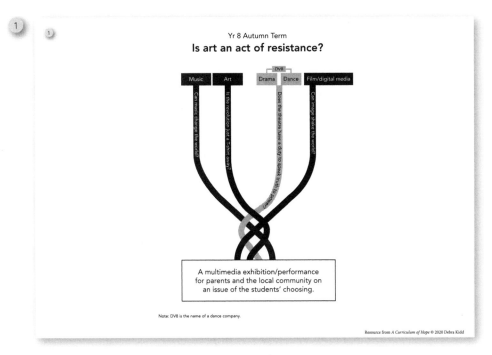

Full size figure can be seen on page 141.
The resource is available to download from www.crownhouse.co.uk/featured/curriculum-hope

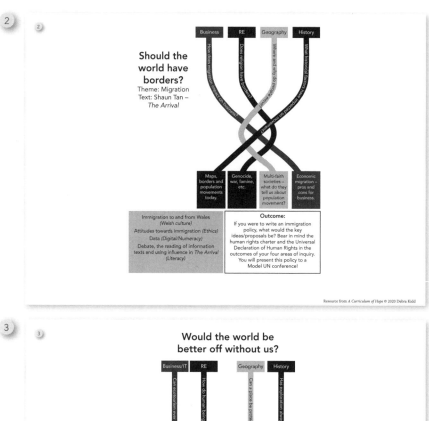

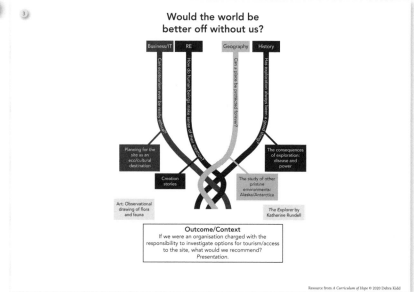

These figures can be seen in full size on pages 142 (Resource 2) and 143 (Resource 3). They are available to download from www.crownhouse.co.uk/featured/curriculum-hope

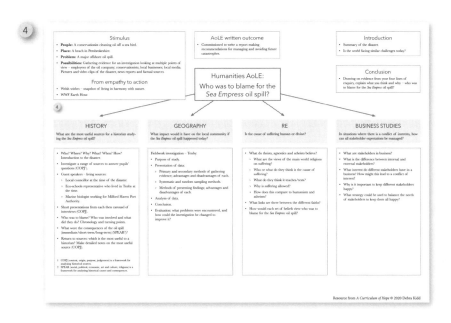

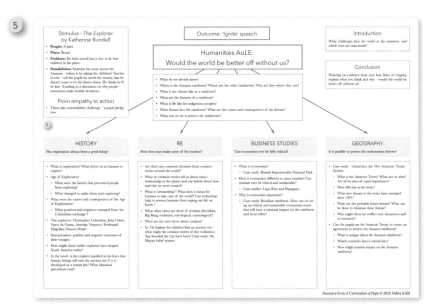

These figures can be seen in full size on pages 144–145 (Resource 4) and 146–147 (Resource 5). They are available to download from www.crownhouse.co.uk/featured/curriculum-hope

From plaiting the questions, we moved on to creating medium-term plans across each AoLE – there is an example below from the expressive arts team for Year 7 (see Resource 7 on pages 150–152 for the Year 8 version). The units allow each subject to deliver its intended theoretical or skills-based content, but to link through inquiry and outcome. In a similar way, the units create links across to other areas of learning and experience without imposing on them or restricting them.

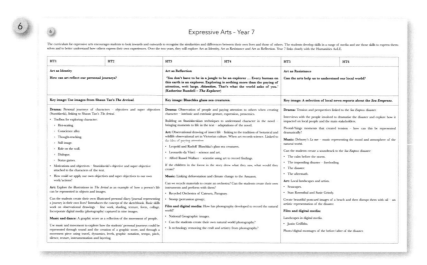

Full size figure can be seen on pages 148–149.
The resource is available to download from www.crownhouse.co.uk/featured/curriculum-hope

St Ebbe's

The examples offered here of medium-term plans from St Ebbe's school in Oxford show how the five C's of credibility (or content – the school chose to make this change because they felt that all the C's were credible and that content better described the place for knowledge), creativity, coherence, compassion and community can be woven into an overview of planning. There are an example for foundation stage, Year 3 and Year 6, as well as a more detailed breakdown of the process for the Year 3 unit.

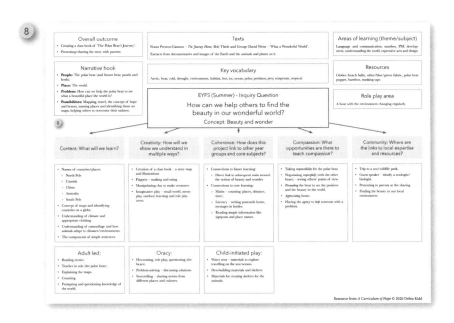

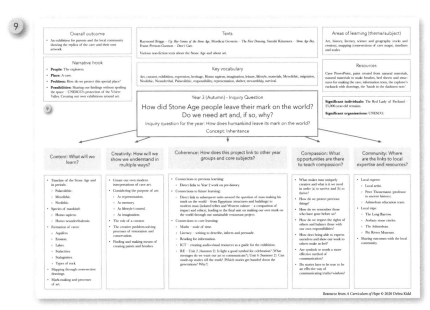

These figures can be seen in full size on pages 154–155 (Resource 8) and 156–157 (Resource 9). They are available to download from www.crownhouse.co.uk/featured/curriculum-hope

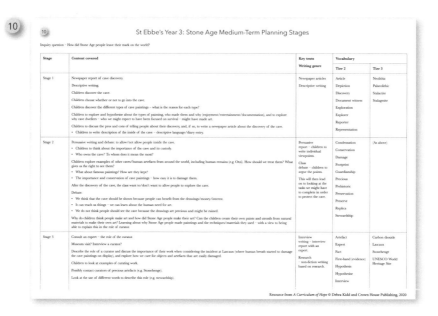

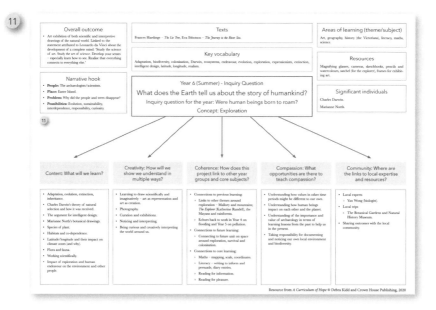

These figures can be seen in full size on pages 158–162 (Resource 10) and 164–165 (Resource 11).
They are available to download from www.crownhouse.co.uk/featured/curriculum-hope

Thorp Primary School

Resource 12 offers an example of how the whole-school year looks when broken down into the units that the school has decided to teach in timed blocks regardless of holiday dates.

- Autumn – eight weeks.

- Second World War (whole school) – three weeks.

- Christmas unit (whole school) – four–five weeks.

- Spring – eight weeks.

- Spring into summer – eight weeks.

- Summer – eight weeks.

It also offers an example of how key elements of geography are being mapped through the year groups to ensure progression of skills and knowledge.

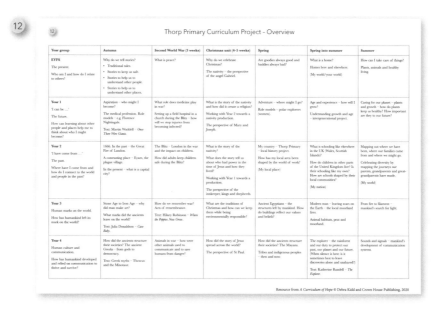

Full size figure can be seen on pages 167–174.

The resource is available to download from www.crownhouse.co.uk/featured/curriculum-hope

Ledbury Primary School

These planning documents are in a similar style to those from St Ebbe's and show examples of how another school is approaching the five C's planning tool.

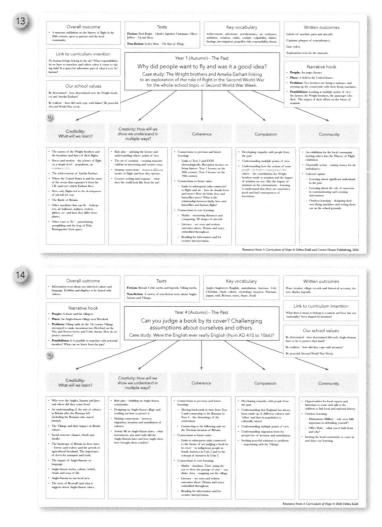

These figures can be seen in full size on pages 176–177 (Resource 13) and 178–179 (Resource 14). They are available to download from www.crownhouse.co.uk/featured/curriculum-hope

Yr 8 Autumn Term
Is art an act of resistance?

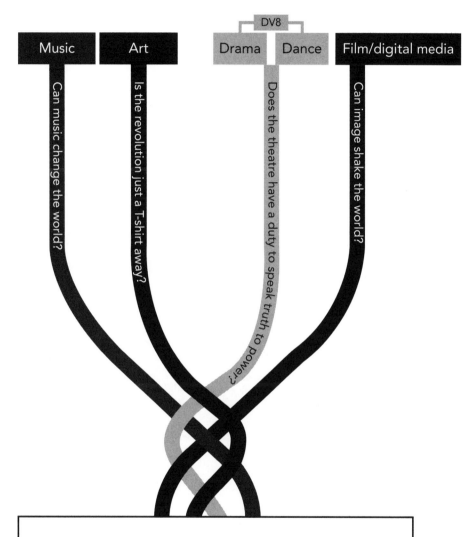

Music

Art

DV8

Drama   Dance

Film/digital media

Can music change the world?

Is the revolution just a T-shirt away?

Does the theatre have a duty to speak truth to power?

Can image shake the world?

A multimedia exhibition/performance
for parents and the local community on
an issue of the students' choosing.

Note: DV8 is the name of a dance company.

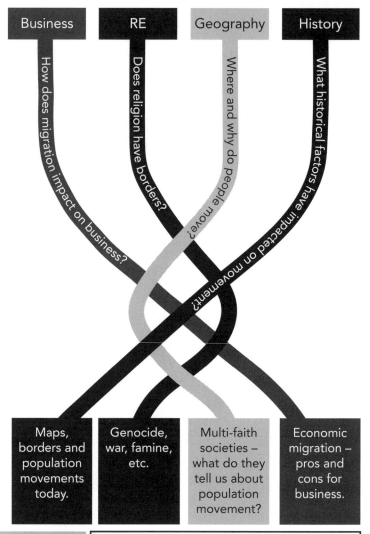

Should the world have borders?

Theme: Migration
Text: Shaun Tan –
The Arrival

Immigration to and from Wales
(Welsh culture)

Attitudes towards immigration *(Ethics)*

Data *(Digital/Numeracy)*

Debate, the reading of information
texts and using influence in *The Arrival*
(Literacy)

Outcome:

If you were to write an immigration
policy, what would the key
ideas/proposals be? Bear in mind the
human rights charter and the Universal
Declaration of Human Rights in the
outcomes of your four areas of inquiry.
You will present this policy to a
Model UN conference!

Would the world be better off without us?

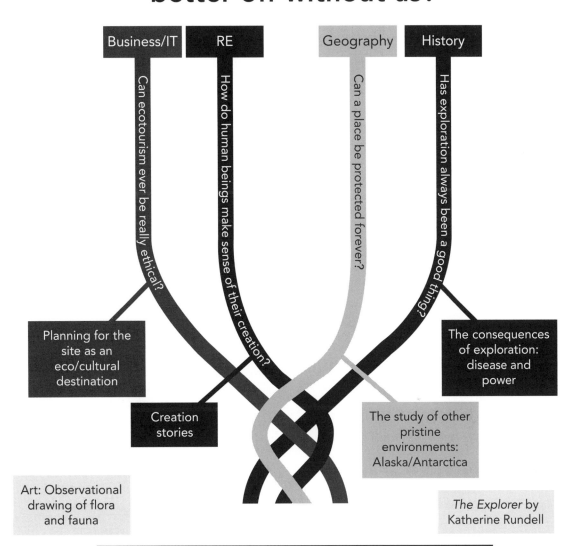

Business/IT — Can ecotourism ever be really ethical?

RE — How do human beings make sense of their creation?

Geography — Can a place be protected forever?

History — Has exploration always been a good thing?

Planning for the site as an eco/cultural destination

Creation stories

The consequences of exploration: disease and power

The study of other pristine environments: Alaska/Antarctica

Art: Observational drawing of flora and fauna

The Explorer by Katherine Rundell

Outcome/Context
If we were an organisation charged with the responsibility to investigate options for tourism/access to the site, what would we recommend?
Presentation.

Stimulus

- **People:** A conservationist cleaning oil off a sea bird.
- **Place:** A beach in Pembrokeshire.
- **Problem:** A major offshore oil spill.
- **Possibilities:** Gathering evidence for an investigation looking at multiple points of view – employees of the oil company; conservationists; local businesses; local media. Pictures and video clips of the disaster, news reports and factual sources.

From empathy to action

- Welsh wishes – snapshot of living in harmony with nature.
- WWF Earth Hour.

Humanities AoLE: Who was to blame for the *Sea Empress* oil spill?

HISTORY

What are the most useful sources for a historian studying the *Sea Empress* oil spill?

- Who? Where? Why? What? When? How? Introduction to the disaster.
- Investigate a range of sources to answer pupils' questions (COPJ[1]).
- Guest speakers – living sources:
  » Local councillor at the time of the disaster.
  » Eco-schools representative who lived in Tenby at the time.
  » Marine biologist working for Milford Haven Port Authority.
- Short presentations from each then carousel of interviews (COPJ).
- Who was to blame? Who was involved and what did they do? Chronology and turning points.
- What were the consequences of the oil spill (immediate/short-term/long-term) (SPEAR[2])?
- Return to sources: which is the most useful to a historian? Make detailed notes on the most useful source (COPJ).

....

1 COPJ (content, origin, purpose, judgement) is a framework for analysing historical sources.
2 SPEAR (social, political, economic, art and culture, religions) is a framework for analysing historical causes and consequences.

GEOGRAPHY

What impact would it have on the local community if the *Sea Empress* oil spill happened today?

Fieldwork investigation – Tenby:

- Purpose of study.
- Presentation of data:
  » Primary and secondary methods of gathering evidence; advantages and disadvantages of each.
  » Systematic and random sampling methods.
  » Methods of presenting findings; advantages and disadvantages of each.
- Analysis of data.
- Conclusion.
- Evaluation: what problems were encountered, and how could the investigation be changed to improve it?

AoLE written outcome

- Commissioned to write a report making recommendations for managing and avoiding future catastrophes.

Introduction

- Summary of the disaster.
- Is the world facing similar challenges today?

Conclusion

- Drawing on evidence from your four lines of enquiry, explain what you think and why – who was to blame for the *Sea Empress* oil spill?

RE

Is the cause of suffering human or divine?

- What do theists, agnostics and atheists believe?
  - » What are the views of the main world religions on suffering?
  - » Who or what do they think is the cause of suffering?
  - » What do they think it teaches/tests?
  - » Why is suffering allowed?
  - » How does this compare to humanism and atheism?
- What links are there between the different faiths?
- How would each set of beliefs view who was to blame for the *Sea Empress* oil spill?

BUSINESS STUDIES

In situations where there is a conflict of interests, how can all stakeholder expectations be managed?

- What are stakeholders in business?
- What is the difference between internal and external stakeholders?
- What interest do different stakeholders have in a business? How might this lead to a conflict of interest?
- Why is it important to keep different stakeholders happy?
- What strategy could be used to balance the needs of stakeholders to keep them all happy?

Stimulus – *The Explorer*
by Katherine Rundell

- **People:** A pilot.
- **Place:** Brazil.
- **Problem:** He feels unwell but is due to fly four children in his plane.
- **Possibilities:** Examine his route across the Amazon – where is he taking the children? Teacher in role – tell the pupils he needs the money, that he doesn't want to let his clients down. He thinks he'll be fine. (Leading to a discussion on why people sometimes make foolish decisions.)

From empathy to action

- Thirty-day sustainability challenge – a pupil pledge tree.

Outcome: 'Ignite' speech

Humanities AoLE:
Would the world be better off without us?

HISTORY

Has exploration always been a good thing?

- What is exploration? What drives us as humans to explore?
- Age of Exploration:
  » What were the factors that prevented people from exploring?
  » What changed to make them start exploring?
- What were the causes and consequences of the Age of Exploration?
  » What positives and negatives emerged from 'the Columbian exchange'?
- The explorers: Christopher Columbus, John Cabot, Vasco da Gama, Amerigo Vespucci, Ferdinand Magellan, Francis Drake.
- Interpretation: positive and negative outcomes of their voyages.
- How might these earlier explorers have shaped South America today?
- In the novel, is the explorer justified in his fears that human beings will ruin the ancient site if it is developed as a tourist site? What historical precedents exist?

RE

How does man make sense of his creation?

- Are there any common elements from creation stories around the world?
- What do creation stories tell us about man's relationship to the planet and our beliefs about how and why we were created?
- What is 'stewardship'? What does it mean for humans to take care of the world? Can technology help to prevent humans from wiping out life on Earth ?
- What other views are there of creation (literalism, Big Bang, evolution, teleological, cosmological)?
- What are my own views about creation?
- In *The Explorer* the children find an ancient city – what might the creation stories of the civilisation that founded the city have been? Case study: the Mayan belief system.

- What do we already know?
- Where is the Amazon rainforest? Where are the other rainforests? Why are they where they are?
- What is the climate like in a rainforest?
- What are the features of a rainforest?
- What is life like for indigenous peoples?
- What threats face the rainforest? What are the causes and consequences of the threats?
- What can we do to protect the rainforests?

Introduction

What challenges face the world at the moment, and which ones are man-made?

Conclusion

Drawing on evidence from your four lines of enquiry, explain what you think and why – would the world be better off without us?

BUSINESS STUDIES

Can ecotourism ever be fully ethical?

- What is ecotourism?
  - » Case study: Bwindi Impenetrable National Park.
- How is ecotourism different to mass tourism? Can tourism ever be ethical and sustainable?
  - » Case studies: Lapa Rios and Papagaya.
- Why is ecotourism important?
  - » Case study: Brazilian rainforest. How can we set up an ethical and sustainable ecotourism resort that will have a minimal impact on the rainforest and local tribes?

GEOGRAPHY

Is it possible to protect the environment forever?

- Case study – Antarctica: the 1961 Antarctic Treaty System:
  - » What is the Antarctic Treaty? What are its aims? Are all its aims of equal importance?
  - » How effective is the treaty?
  - » What new threats to the treaty have emerged since 1961?
  - » What are the probable future threats? What can be done to minimise these threats?
  - » Why might there be conflict over Antarctica and its resources?
- Can the pupils use the Antarctic Treaty to create an agreement to protect the Amazon rainforest?
  - » What is unique about the Amazon rainforest?
  - » Which countries does it extend into?
  - » How might tourism impact on the Amazon rainforest?

Expressive Arts – Year 7

The curriculum for expressive arts encourages students to look inwards and outwards to recognise the similarities and differences between their own lives and those of others. The students develop skills in a range of media and use those skills to express themselves and to better understand how others express their own experiences. Over the two years, they will explore Art as Identity, Art as Resistance and Art as Reflection. Year 7 links closely with the Humanities AoLE.

HT1	HT2	HT3	HT4	HT5	HT6
Art as Identity		**Art as Reflection**		**Art as Resistance**	
How can art reflect our personal journeys?		**'You don't have to be in a jungle to be an explorer ... Every human on this earth is an explorer. Exploring is nothing more than the paying of attention, writ large. *Attention.* That's what the world asks of you.'** (Katherine Rundell – *The Explorer*)		**Can the arts help us to understand our local world?**	
Key image: Use images from Shaun Tan's *The Arrival.*		**Key image: Blaschka glass sea creatures.**		**Key image: A selection of local news reports about the *Sea Empress*.**	
Drama: Personal journeys of characters – objectives and super objectives (Stanislavski), linking to Shaun Tan's *The Arrival*. • Toolbox for exploring character: » Hot-seating. » Conscience alley » Thought-tracking. » Still image. » Role on the wall.		**Drama:** Observation of people and pay-ing attention to others when creating character – intrinsic and extrinsic gesture, expression, proxemics. Building on Stanislavskian techniques to understand character in the novel – bring-ing moments to life in the text – adaptations of the novel. **Art:** Observational drawing of insect life – linking to the tradition of botanical and wildlife observational art in Victorian		**Drama:** Tension and perspectives linked to the *Sea Empress* disaster. Interviews with the people involved to dramatise the disaster and explore how it impacted on local people and the main stakeholders. Pivotal/hinge moments that created ten-sion – how can this be represented dramatically?	

» Status games.

- Motivations and objectives – Stanislavski's objective and super objective attached to the characters of the text.

- How could we apply our own objectives and super objectives to our own work/actions?

Art: Explore the illustrations in *The Arrival* as an example of how a person's life can be represented in objects and images.

Can the students create their own illustrated personal diary/journal representing a journey in their own lives? Introduces the concept of the sketchbook. Basic skills work on observational drawings – line work, shading, texture, form, collage. Incorporate digital media (photography) captured in nine images.

Music and dance: A graphic score as a reflection of the movement of people.

Use music and movement to explore how the students' personal journeys could be represented through sound and the creation of a graphic score, and through a movement piece using travel, dynamics, levels, graphic notation, tempo, pitch, silence, texture, instrumentation and layering.

---

to the idea of paying attention.

- Leopold and Rudolf Blaschka's glass sea creatures.

- Leonardo da Vinci – science and art.

- Alfred Russel Wallace – scientist using art to record findings.

If the children in the forest in the story drew what they saw, what would they create?

Music: Linking deforestation and climate change to the Amazon.

Can we recycle materials to create an orchestra? Can the students create their own instruments and perform with them?

- Recycled Orchestra of Cateura, Paraguay.

- Stomp (percussion group).

Film and digital media: How has photography developed to record the natural world?

- National Geographic images.

- Can the students create their own natural world photography?

- Is technology removing the craft and artistry from photography?

---

senting the mood and atmosphere of the natural world.

Can the students create a soundtrack to the *Sea Empress* disaster:

- The calm before the storm.

- The impending disaster – foreboding.

- The disaster.

- The aftermath.

Art: Local landscapes and artists.

- Seascapes.

- Stan Rosenthal and Susie Grindy.

Create beautiful postcard images of a beach and then disrupt them with oil – an artistic representation of the disaster.

Film and digital media:

Landscapes in digital media.

- Justin Griffiths.

Photo/digital montages of the before/after of the disaster.

Expressive Arts – Year 8

HT1	HT2	HT3	HT4	HT5	HT6
Art as Resistance		**Art as Identity**		**Art as Reflection**	
Is art an act of resistance?		What makes us who we are?		Is art a reflection of society?	
Key image: Bansky – *Mobile Lovers*		Key image: Hundertwasser – *Irinaland over the Balkans*		Key image: Picasso – *Guernica*	

Drama and dance: Does theatre have a duty to speak truth to power? What forms of protest are available to people who disagree with a decision?

- Peaceful protest.
- Violent protest.
- Economic protest.
- Examples: March for Our Lives, Greta Thunberg/Extinction Rebellion.

How do people protest through the arts?

- Bertolt Brecht (dialectical theatre).
- Augusto Boal (Theatre of the Oppressed).
- DV8 Physical Theatre.
- Attraction (shadow theatre group).
- Dakota & Nadia (domestic violence).
- Capoeira (Brazilian martial art).

Drama and dance: How do we use 'masks' to project our identity to different audiences? How do others perceive us?

- Mask work in theatre (e.g. Trestle Theatre).
- Puppetry to represent others' identity (e.g. Horse + Bamboo).
- Symbolic representation through costume.

Students to create a physical theatre performance utilising masks, puppetry or costumes (or a combination) to explore an issue of their identity.

Visual art: Use Hundertwasser as a stimulus to explore the three 'skins' of identity – skin, clothing, home. Take the idea of skin further to create masks that represent the identity of the creator.

- Use line and colour like Hundertwasser.

Drama and dance: How does theatre disrupt our reflection of society?

- Antonin Artaud and Jerzy Grotowski.

Research into how these theatre directors/theorists reflected the society of their own time using techniques (e.g. non-naturalistic elements) that disrupted how audiences reacted and responded.

How could these techniques be used to create our own reflections of society at a local, national and international level?

Music: How does music reflect society?

- John Cage – 4'33".
- Terry Riley – In C (for performance).
- Stravinsky – The Rite of Spring.
- The Sex Pistols and punk.

- Use Trestle masks to inspire expression.
- Link to drama/dance themes.
- Create their own masks to use in the final performance.

Music: How can music create a sense of identity?

- How do popular music artists use aspects of identity to either show or hide who they are?
- Composition techniques.
- The musical artist as theatrical performer – David Bowie, Lady Gaga, Sia.
- Record something that is used as a soundtrack within their performance.

Film and digital media: Students to create a mood board of photography that represents their identity which can be used as a stimulus for artwork in the other expressive arts areas and which could be used for projection work in the final performance.

Outcome: Physical theatre performance using masks, music and photography to explore the notion of identity.

- How has music disrupted audiences in an attempt to shake society?
- What is music – what does music need to have in order to be music?
- Can we create our own 'disruptive' musical pieces to reflect the state we think our society is in.

Art: How does art record society?

- Picasso – Guernica.

Introducing the context of *Guernica* – a broken society.

Introducing the idea of portraiture – a fractured reflective surface, or a broken object …

What are the fractures in our own society?

- Political.
- Technological/social.
- Climate/consumerism.

How could we create our own artworks that represent and reflect society and our place within it?

Play with ideas in the production of a sketchbook of responses and ideas. Celebrate the sketchbook as an outcome in its own right.

- Devise a piece of theatre using Brechtian and Boalian techniques (or another) to create a piece of political theatre.

Music: Can music change the world? How did blues music develop as a form of protest?

- 'Oh, Freedom' (traditional spiritual); 'Since I've Laid This Burden Down' (Mississippi John Hurt); 'Woman' (Wolfmother).
- The form of blues music.
- Context behind blues music.

Write their own protest songs using 12-bar blues music structures to create a multimedia performance.

Visual art: Is the revolution just a slogan away? Graffiti art and protest.

- Keith Haring and New York street art – transition from protest/alternative art to the mainstream to raise awareness of issues.
- Beatbox and hip-hop (linking and developing from music).
- Graffiti protest through time – evidence from Ancient Rome and Greece.
- Banksy.
- Acts of resistance and the law – should we learn about art that is illegal?

HT1	HT2	HT3	HT4	HT5	HT6
• If we put a monetary value on art designed to resist, is it still protest art? Students to create their own graffiti-style protest art to bring to a multimedia performance. **Film and digital media:** Woven into performing and visual arts via: • Use of digital/projected media in the work of DV8. • Community links with Interfilm. • Use of image projection and shadow puppetry in performance to communicate protest. **Outcome:** Multimedia exhibition/performance for the local community. All groups prepare a performance and artwork, but they can select which art form they want to share publicly.				**Film and digital media:** How can we create our own reflection of our society? • Katie Mitchell's use of projection in performance – surrealism. Create a multimedia resource to demonstrate how the students wish to reflect their own society, linking across AoLEs to the skills they have learned in ICT (e.g. stop-motion animation, video-editing skills).	
Linking theme connecting the two units: Banksy, Hundertwasser and Sia – hiding in plain sight.				**Links back to units on protest and identity.**	
People: A 16-year-old. **Place:** Their bedroom. **Problem:** The government have brought in a law to outlaw technology.		**People:** A 12-year-old. **Place:** A bedroom in Germany in 1940. **Problem:** He is Jewish, pretending to be a Christian boy and getting ready to attend a meeting of the Hitler Youth.		**People:** A 14-year-old. **Place:** A bedroom littered with broken and smashed objects. **Problem:** Frustration with the world – the teenager wants to smash everything up.	

Overall outcome

- Creating a class book of 'The Polar Bear's Journey'.
- Presenting/sharing the story with parents.

Narrative hook

- **People:** The polar bear (and brown bear, panda and koala).
- **Place:** The world.
- **Problem:** How can we help the polar bear to see what a beautiful place the world is?
- **Possibilities:** Mapping, travel, the concept of hope and beauty, naming places and identifying them on maps, helping others to overcome their sadness.

EYFS (Summer) – Inquiry Question

How can we help others to find the beauty in our wonderful world?

Concept: Beauty and wonder

Content: What will we learn?

- Names of countries/places:
  » North Pole
  » Canada
  » China
  » Australia
  » South Pole
- Concept of maps and identifying countries on a globe.
- Understanding of climate and appropriate clothing.
- Understanding of camouflage and how animals adapt to climates/environments.
- The components of simple sentences.

Creativity: How will we show we understand in multiple ways?

- Creation of a class book – a story map and illustrations.
- Puppets – making and using.
- Manipulating clay to make creatures.
- Imaginative play – small world, messy play, outdoor learning and role play areas.

Adult led:

- Reading stories.
- Teacher in role (the polar bear).
- Explaining the maps.
- Counting.
- Prompting and questioning knowledge of the world.

Oracy:

- Hot-seating, role play, questioning (the bears).
- Problem-solving – discussing solutions.
- Storytelling – sharing stories from different places and cultures.

Texts

Frann Preston-Gannon – *The Journey Home*, Bob Thiele and George David Weiss – 'What a Wonderful World'.

Extracts from documentaries and images of the Earth and the animals and plants on it.

Key vocabulary

Arctic, bear, cold, drought, environment, habitat, hot, ice, ocean, polar, predator, prey, temperate, tropical.

Areas of learning (theme/subject)

Language and communication, number, PSE development, understanding the world, expressive arts and design.

Resources

Globes (beach balls), white/blue/green fabric, polar bear puppet, bamboo, masking tape.

Role play area

A boat with the environment changing regularly.

Coherence: How does this project link to other year groups and core subjects?

- Connections to future learning:
  » Direct link to subsequent units around the notion of beauty and wonder.
- Connections to core learning:
  » Maths – counting (places, distance, time).
  » Literacy – writing postcards home, messages in bottles.
  » Reading simple information like signposts and place names.

Compassion: What opportunities are there to teach compassion?

- Taking *responsibility* for the polar bear.
- Negotiating *respectfully* (with the other bears) – seeing others' points of view.
- *Persuading* the bear to see the positives and the beauty in the world.
- *Appreciating* home.
- Having the *agency* to *help* someone with a problem.

Community: Where are the links to local expertise and resources?

- Trip to a zoo/wildlife park.
- Guest speaker – ideally a zoologist/biologist.
- Presenting to parents at the sharing.
- Finding the beauty in our local environment.

Child-initiated play:

- Water area – materials to explore travelling on the sea/oceans.
- Den-building materials and shelters.
- Materials for creating shelters for the animals.

Overall outcome

- An exhibition for parents and the local community showing the replica of the cave and their own artwork.

Narrative hook

- **People:** The explorers.
- **Place:** A cave.
- **Problem:** How do we protect this special place?
- **Possibilities:** Sharing our findings without spoiling the space – UNESCO's protection of the Vésère Valley. Creating our own exhibitions around art.

Year 3 (Autumn) - Inquiry Question

How did Stone Age people leave their mark on the world? Do we need art and, if so, why?

Inquiry question for the year: How does humankind leave its mark on the world?

Concept: Inheritance

Content: What will we learn?

- Timeline of the Stone Age and its periods:
  » Palaeolithic.
  » Mesolithic.
  » Neolithic.
- Species of mankind:
  » Homo sapiens.
  » Homo neanderthalensis.
- Formation of caves:
  » Aquifers.
  » Erosion.
  » Lakes.
  » Stalactites.
  » Stalagmites.
  » Types of rock.
- Mapping through cross-section drawings.
- Mark-making and processes of art.

Coherence: How does this project link to other year groups and core subjects?

- Connections to previous learning:
  » Direct links to Year 2 work on pre-history.
- Connections to future learning:
  » Direct link to subsequent units around the question of man making his mark on the world – from Egyptians (structures and buildings) to modern man (isolated tribes and Western culture – a comparison of impact and ethics), leading to the final unit on making our own mark on the world through our sustainable restaurant project.
- Connections to core learning:
  » Maths – scale of time.
  » Literacy – writing to describe, inform and persuade.
  » Reading for information.
  » ICT – creating audio-visual resources as a guide for the exhibition.
  » RE – Unit 2 (Autumn 2): Is light a good symbol for celebration? (What messages do we want our art to communicate?); Unit 6 (Summer 2): Can made-up stories tell the truth? (Which stories get handed down the generations? Why?)

Texts

Raymond Briggs – *Ug: Boy Genius of the Stone Age*, Mordicai Gerstein – *The First Drawing*, Satoshi Kitamura – *Stone Age Boy*, Frann Preston-Gannon – *Dave's Cave*.

Various non-fiction texts about the Stone Age and about art.

Key vocabulary

Art, curator, exhibition, expression, heritage, Homo sapiens, imagination, leisure, lifestyle, materials, Mesolithic, migration, Neolithic, Neanderthal, Palaeolithic, responsibility, representation, shelter, stewardship, survival.

Areas of learning (theme/subject)

Art, history, literacy, science and geography (rocks and erosion), mapping (cross-sections of cave maps), timelines and scales.

Resources

Cave PowerPoint, paint created from natural materials, natural materials to make brushes, bed sheets and structures for making the cave, information texts, the explorer's rucksack with drawings, the 'hands in the darkness note'.

Significant individuals: The Red Lady of Paviland – 25,000-year-old remains.

Significant organisations: UNESCO.

Creativity: How will we show we understand in multiple ways?

- Create our own modern interpretations of cave art.
- Considering the purpose of art:
  » As representation.
  » As memory.
  » As lifestyle/control.
  » As imagination.
- The role of a curator.
- The creative problem-solving processes of restoration and conservation.
- Finding and making means of creating paints and brushes.

Compassion: What opportunities are there to teach compassion?

- What makes man uniquely creative and what is it we need in order (a) to survive and (b) to thrive?
- How do we protect precious things?
- How do we remember those who have gone before us?
- How do we respect the rights of others and balance those with our own responsibilities?
- How does being able to express ourselves and show our work to others make us feel?
- Are symbols or words a more effective method of communication?
- Do stories have to be true to be an effective way of communicating truths/wisdom?

Community: Where are the links to local expertise and resources?

- Local experts:
  » Local artist.
  » Peter Thonemann (professor in ancient history).
  » Ashmolean education team.
- Local trips:
  » The Long Barrow.
  » Avebury stone circles.
  » The Ashmolean.
  » Pitt Rivers Museum.
- Sharing outcomes with the local community.

10

St Ebbe's Year 3: Stone Age Medium-Term Planning Stages

Inquiry question – How did Stone Age people leave their mark on the world?

Stage	Content covered	Key texts	Vocabulary	
		Writing genre	Tier 2	Tier 3
Stage 1	Newspaper report of cave discovery.	Newspaper articles	Article	Neolithic
	Descriptive writing.	Descriptive writing	Depiction	Palaeolithic
	Children discover the cave.		Discovery	Stalactite
	Children choose whether or not to go into the cave.		Document witness	Stalagmite
	Children discover the different types of cave paintings – what is the reason for each type?		Exploration	
	Children to explore and hypothesise about the types of painting, who made them and why (enjoyment/entertainment/documentation), and to explore why cave dwellers – who we might expect to have been focused on survival – might have made art.		Explorer	
			Reporter	
	Children to discuss the pros and cons of telling people about their discovery, and, if so, to write a newspaper article about the discovery of the cave.		Representation	
	• Children to write description of the inside of the cave – descriptive language/diary entry.			

Stage 2		Persuasive report – children to write individual viewpoints. Class debate – children to argue the points. This will then lead on to looking at the tasks we might have to complete in order to protect the cave.	Condensation Conservation Damage Footprint Guardianship Precious Prehistoric Preservation Preserve Replica Stewardship	(As above)
	Persuasive writing and debate: to allow/not allow people inside the cave. • Children to think about the importance of the cave and its custody. • Who owns the cave? To whom does it mean the most? Children explore examples of other caves/human artefacts from around the world, including human remains (e.g. Otzi). How should we treat them? What gives us the right to see them? • What about famous paintings? How are they kept? • The importance and conservation of cave paintings – how easy it is to damage them. After the discovery of the cave, the class want to/don't want to allow people to explore the cave. Debate: • We think that the cave should be shown because people can benefit from the drawings/money/interest. • It can teach us things – we can learn about the human need for art. • We do not think people should see the cave because the drawings are precious and might be ruined. Why do children think people make art and how did Stone Age people make their art? Can the children create their own paints and utensils from natural materials to make their own art? Learning about why Stone Age people made paintings and the techniques/materials they used – with a view to being able to explain this in the role of curator.			

159

Stage	Content covered	Key texts	Vocabulary	
		Writing genre	Tier 2	Tier 3
Stage 3	Consult an expert – the role of the curator. Museum visit? Interview a curator? Describe the role of a curator and discuss the importance of their work when considering the incident at Lascaux (where human breath started to damage the cave paintings on display), and explore how we care for objects and artefacts that are easily damaged. Children to look at examples of curating work. Possibly contact curators of precious artefacts (e.g. Stonehenge). Look at the use of different words to describe this role (e.g. stewardship). Research an area of Stone Age life in preparation for our exhibition.	Interview writing – interview report with an expert. Research – non-fiction writing based on research.	Artefact Expert Fact First-hand (evidence) Hypothesis Hypothesise Interview Interviewee Interviewer Second-hand (evidence) Theory	Carbon dioxide Lascaux Stonehenge UNESCO World Heritage Site

Stage 4	Non-fiction explanation writing – creating a museum plaque. Children to use their knowledge of the cave and why the paintings are there. Children to write a museum information panel using information about their own painting.	Creating information leaflets Museum wall plaques	Age (BC etc.) Carbon dating Dating Expertise Explanation Guardian Information Knowledge Leaflet Steward	(As above)
Stage 5	Invitation writing – before the cave is replicated for the parents. Children to create resources and invitations. Oral storytelling.	Myths/legends – use paintings for inspiration for mythical storytelling Shadow puppet shows	Attendance Attendee (linked to interviewee) Guardian Invitation Legend Letter Mark-making Myth	(As above)

Stage	Content covered	Key texts	Vocabulary	
		Writing genre	Tier 2	Tier 3
Stage 6	Invitation to see the cave. Tour guides. Repetition of tour to parents/community/other classes. Repetition of knowledge.	Information texts and signage	(As above)	(As above)

11

Overall outcome

- Art exhibition of both scientific and interpretive drawings of the natural world. Linked to the statement attributed to Leonardo da Vinci about the development of a complete mind: 'Study the science of art. Study the art of science. Develop your senses – especially learn how to see. Realise that everything connects to everything else.'

Narrative hook

- **People:** The archaeologists/scientists.
- **Place:** Easter Island.
- **Problem:** Why did the people and trees disappear?
- **Possibilities:** Evolution, sustainability, interdependence, responsibility, curiosity.

Year 6 (Summer) – Inquiry Question

What does the Earth tell us about the story of humankind?

Inquiry question for the year: Were human beings born to roam?

Concept: Exploration

Content: What will we learn?

- Adaptation, evolution, extinction, inheritance.
- Charles Darwin's theory of natural selection and how it was received.
- The argument for intelligent design.
- Marianne North's botanical drawings.
- Species of plant.
- Habitats and co-dependence.
- Latitude/longitude and their impact on climate zones (and why).
- Flora and fauna.
- Working scientifically.
- Impact of exploration and human endeavour on the environment and other people.

Coherence: How does this project link to other year groups and core subjects?

- Connections to previous learning:
  - » Links to other themes around exploration – Mallory and mountains; *The Explorer* (Katherine Rundell), the Mayans and rainforests.
  - » Echoes back to work in Year 4 on flooding and Year 5 on pollution.
- Connections to future learning:
  - » Connecting to future unit on space around exploration, survival and colonisation.
- Connections to core learning:
  - » Maths – mapping, scale, coordinates.
  - » Literacy – writing to inform and persuade, diary entries.
  - » Reading for information.
  - » Reading for pleasure.

Texts

Frances Hardinge – *The Lie Tree*, Eva Ibbotson – *The Journey to the River Sea*.

Areas of learning (theme/subject)

Art, geography, history (the Victorians), literacy, maths, science.

Key vocabulary

Adaptation, biodiversity, colonisation, Darwin, ecosystems, endeavour, evolution, exploration, expressionism, extinction, intelligent design, latitude, longitude, realism.

Resources

Magnifying glasses, cameras, sketchbooks, pencils and watercolours, satchel (for the explorer), frames for exhibiting art.

Significant individuals

Charles Darwin.

Marianne North.

Creativity: How will we show we understand in multiple ways?

- Learning to draw scientifically and imaginatively – art as representation and art as creation.
- Photography.
- Curation and exhibitions.
- Noticing and interpreting.
- Being curious and creatively interpreting the world around us.

Compassion: What opportunities are there to teach compassion?

- Understanding how values in other time periods might be different to our own.
- Understanding how human beings impact on each other and the planet.
- Understanding of the importance and value of archaeology in terms of learning lessons from the past to help us in the present.
- Taking responsibility for documenting and noticing our own local environment and biodiversity.

Community: Where are the links to local expertise and resources?

- Local experts
  » Yan Wong (biologist).
- Local trips
  » The Botanical Gardens and Natural History Museum.
- Sharing outcomes with the local community.

Thorp Primary Curriculum Project – Overview

Year group	Autumn	Second World War (3 weeks)	Christmas unit (4–5 weeks)	Spring	Spring into summer	Summer
EYFS The present. Who am I and how do I relate to others?	Why do we tell stories? • Traditional tales. • Stories to keep us safe. • Stories to help us to understand other people. • Stories to help us to understand other places.	What is peace?	Why do we celebrate Christmas? The nativity – the perspective of the angel Gabriel.	Are goodies always good and baddies always bad?	What is a home? Homes here and elsewhere. (My world/your world)	How can I take care of things? Plants, animals and healthy living.

Year group	Autumn	Second World War (3 weeks)	Christmas unit (4–5 weeks)	Spring	Spring into summer	Summer
Year 1 'I can be …'. The future. How can learning about other people and places help me to think about who I might become?	Aspiration – who might I become? The medical profession. Role models – e.g. Florence Nightingale. Text: Martin Waddell – *Once There Were Giants*.	What role does medicine play in war? Setting up a field hospital in a church during the Blitz – how will we stop injuries from becoming infected?	What is the story of the nativity and how did it create a religion? Working with Year 2 towards a nativity production. The perspective of Mary and Joseph.	Adventure – where might I go? Role models – polar explorers (women).	Age and experience – how will I grow? Understanding growth and age – intergenerational project.	Caring for our planet – plants and growth – how do plants keep us healthy? How important are they to our future?
Year 2 'I have come from …'. The past. Where have I come from and how do I connect to the world and people in the past?	1666. In the past – the Great Fire of London. A contrasting place – Eyam, the plague village. In the present – what is a capital city?	The Blitz – London in the war and the impact on children. How did adults keep children safe during the Blitz?	What is the story of the nativity? What does the story tell us about who had power in the time of Jesus and how they lived? Working with Year 1 towards a production. The perspective of the innkeeper, kings and shepherds.	My country – Thorp Primary – local history project. How has my local area been shaped by the world of work? (My local place)	What is schooling like elsewhere in the UK (Wales, Scottish Islands)? How do children in other parts of the United Kingdom live? Is their schooling like my own? How are schools shaped by their local communities? (My nation)	Mapping out where we have been, where our families came from and where we might go. Celebrating diversity by mapping the journeys our parents, grandparents and great-grandparents have made. (My world)

Year 3 Human marks on the world. How has humankind left its mark on the world?	Stone Age to Iron Age – why did man make art? What marks did the ancients leave on the world? Text: Julia Donaldson – *Cave Baby*.	How do we remember war? Acts of remembrance. Text: Hilary Robinson – *Where the Poppies Now Grow*.	What are the traditions of Christmas and how can we keep them while being environmentally responsible?	Ancient Egyptians – the structures left by mankind. How do buildings reflect our values and beliefs?	Modern man – leaving scars on the Earth – the local moorland fires. Animal habitats, peat and moorland.	From fire to filament – mankind's search for light.

169

Year group	Autumn	Second World War (3 weeks)	Christmas unit (4–5 weeks)	Spring	Spring into summer	Summer
Year 4 Human culture and communication. How has humankind developed and relied on communication to thrive and survive?	How did the ancients structure their societies? The ancient Greeks – from gods to democracy. Text: Greek myths – Theseus and the Minotaur.	Animals in war – how were other animals used to communicate and to save humans from danger?	How did the story of Jesus spread across the world? The perspective of St Paul.	How did the ancients structure their societies? The Mayans. Tribes and indigenous peoples – then and now.	The explorer – the rainforest and our duty to protect our past, our planet and our future. (When silence is best: is it sometimes best to leave discoveries alone and unshared?) Text: Katherine Rundell – *The Explorer*.	Sounds and signals – mankind's development of communication systems.
Year 5 Human endeavour. How have human beings overcome adversity?	Exploration in the past – has exploration always been a good thing?	Bravery in war – the resistance. How have human beings overcome adversity in wartime?	Continuation of Second World War. Text: Michelle Magorian – *Goodnight Mister Tom*. How did people celebrate Christmas in wartime?	Natural disasters – earthquakes and volcanoes. How does mankind cope with the movements of the Earth? Link to Pompeii to introduce the Romans.	Our cultural melting pot – from Romans to Normans – the influences that have shaped Britain. Causes of migration through invasion.	Space exploration – frontiers of the future.

Year 6	Responsibility for each other.	Learning lessons from war	Consumerism and Christmas.	Responsibility for our planet.	Responsibility for others – migration and refugees.	Responsibility for ourselves – moving to secondary school.
Human responsibility. Does man really have dominion over the Earth?	Plots and protests – from Peterloo to the climate strikes …	how do we make sure it never happens again?	Has the Christmas message been lost? Perspective – the homeless and people in poverty.	Water – the image of the boys on the roof in Bangladesh as a stimulus. The nature crisis – from evolution to extinction.		

Threading skills through the curriculum – example – skills in geography:

	EYFS	Year 1	Year 2	Year 3	Year 4	Year 5	Year 6
Mapping	Mapping stories – story maps with symbols. Building the concept of maps and aerial views. Understanding the concept that a map is a 2D	Interior maps and floor plans – simple sketches – for example, the hospital in the Second World War unit. Directions – up, down, left, right. Mapping our local area	Map of the UK – how are country maps coded? – the journey from London to Eyam (Unit 1), the cities of the Blitz (Unit 2), etc. Directions and compass points	Cross-sections and elevations – cave elevations and maps (Unit 1) and cross-sections of Egyptian tombs (Unit 3). Simple grids and symbols on maps – rivers, etc.	Topographical features on a map – the Amazon and using four-figure grid references on a map of the area. Mapping the children's locations in *The Explorer*.	How maps of the world emerged through exploration – comparing maps of the past to the present (Unit 3) and maps as globes (Unit 4). Comparing types of map	Mapping migration – how has the movement of people shaped maps and borders? How has war shaped maps and borders? How do people who are lost at sea know their locations?

	EYFS	Year 1	Year 2	Year 3	Year 4	Year 5	Year 6
Mapping	representation of a place using symbols.	– where is our school in relation to other significant places of work in the area? Mapping places of work on a simple local map.	– north, south, east, west.	Local Ordnance Survey map – local moorland fire (Unit 3). First look at four-point grid referencing; Compass points (north, south, east, west) and how to read a map. How to read a map to find your way and use a compass to help you.	The equator on maps. Contours on maps and revisit four-point grid referencing. Using compass points to plot a way out of the forest using the eight points of the compass.	– revisit Ordnance Survey maps vs. global maps. Using compass points to circumnavigate the globe – introducing latitude and longitude.	know their locations? Linking compass points to latitude/longitude/ Global Positioning System (GPS) and six-figure grid referencing.
People (social)	Where do people live and why do they need homes? Concept of living in a place and comparisons to where others live.	Why might people move for work and where might they go? Migration (for work).	Urban and rural – London and Eyam and the Blitz – how does where we live impact on how we deal with disaster, and why might we have to move?	From gathering to farming – using the land for agriculture (Stone Age) and for fuel (moorland and peat).	The movement of belief systems and how Christianity spread across the world.	Migration through invasion over time vs. migration through exploration.	Impact of nature on human settlements – rivers, flooding, natural disasters, etc.

Place – topographical	Naming features (in story settings) – river, forest, path, cave, village, etc.	Ice caps and poles. Icebergs. Names of continents and oceans.	Urban and rural/cities and villages. How did topography affect Eyam or London during the Great Fire?	Moorland environments. Caves (including the formation of stalactites and stalagmites).	Rainforests – rivers (the Amazon).	Volcanoes and tectonic plates – their impact on settlements.	Rivers and coasts.
Location knowledge	Identifying Royton on a map of the UK and identifying India on a map (Unit 3).	The Arctic and countries in the Arctic (Unit 2). Naming the Arctic Ocean and the Arctic and Antarctic continents.	Local area – Royton and Thorp, London and Eyam. The countries of the UK (comparing schools and education), their capital cities and regions.	Stonehenge and other Stone/Bronze Age sites – identifying them on a map and looking at how ancient sites are marked on a map. Egypt. Local location knowledge – Saddleworth Moor.	The Amazon river and the countries it flows through, and countries that contain the Amazon rainforest. Identifying South America on a map.	Countries in Europe and their imprint on the rest of the world through early exploration. Former colonies. Countries of the Roman empire.	Manchester. Bangladesh. Local knowledge (the river). The Galápagos Islands.

	EYFS	Year 1	Year 2	Year 3	Year 4	Year 5	Year 6
Climate and weather	Wearing clothing appropriate to the weather – naming weather (rain, snow, sunshine, etc.). Impact of weather on plants and animals.	Cold weather and snow – impact on polar explorers (Unit 2) (seasons are taught throughout the year at the appropriate time).	Temperate climate zone (our local climate) – the water cycle – the impact of the Atlantic Ocean on our climate.	Desert climate zone (Egypt) and how weather impacted on the preservation of bodies and on the need for irrigation.	Tropical climate zones.	Impact of a volcanic explosion on weather – Krakatoa and Tambora.	Peterloo – the rise of protest after the Tambora eruption led to global crop failures.

13

Overall outcome

- A museum exhibition on the history of flight in the 20th century, open to parents and the local community.

Link to curriculum intention

Do human beings belong in the air? What responsibilities do we have to ourselves and others when it comes to taking risks? Is a quest for adventure part of what it is to 'be' human?

Our school values

Be determined – how determined were the Wright brothers and Amelia Earhart?

Be resilient – how did each cope with failure? Be peaceful (Second World War week).

Year 1 (Autumn) – The Past

Why did people want to fly and was it a good idea?

Case study: The Wright brothers and Amelia Earhart linking to an exploration of the role of flight in the Second World War for the whole-school topic in Second World War Week.

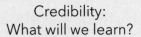

Credibility: What will we learn?

- The names of the Wright brothers and the locations and dates of their flights.
- Forces and motion – the science of flight (at a simple level – propulsion, air resistance, etc.).
- The achievements of Amelia Earhart.
- Where the United States is and the name of the ocean that separates it from the UK (and over which Earhart flew).
- How early flights led to the development of aircraft for war.
- The Battle of Britain.
- Other machines that can fly – helicopters, air balloons, zephyrs, rockets, gliders, etc. and how they differ from planes.
- Other ways to 'fly' – parachuting, paragliding and the leap of Felix Baumgartner from space.

Coherence

- Connections to previous and future learning:
  - » Links to Year 2 and EYFS chronologically: Reception focuses on living history; Year 1 focuses on the 20th century; Year 2 focuses on the 19th century.
- Connections to future units:
  - » Links to subsequent units connected to flight and air – how do clouds form and move? How do birds, bees and butterflies move? What is the relationship between birds, bees and butterflies and human flight?
- Connections to core learning:
  - » Maths – measuring distances and comparing. 3D shapes of aircraft.
  - » Literacy – see texts and written outcomes above. Drama and oracy embedded throughout.
  - » Reading for information and for creative interpretation.

Key vocabulary

Achievement, adventure, aerodynamics, air resistance, ambition, aviation, cabin, cockpit, culpability, failure, fuselage, investigation, propeller, risk, responsibility, thrust.

Written outcomes

Labels (of machine parts and aircraft).

Captions (plaques of remembrance).

Lists (rules).

Explanation texts for the museum.

Texts

Fiction: Paul Bright – *Charlie's Superhero Underpants*, Oliver Jeffers – *Up and Down*.

Non-fiction: Lesley Sims – *The Story of Flying*.

Narrative hook

- **People:** An angry farmer.
- **Place:** A field in the United States.
- **Problem:** Two brothers are being a nuisance and messing up the countryside with their flying machines.
- **Possibilities:** Looking at multiple points of view – the farmer, the Wright brothers, the passenger who died. The impact of their efforts on the future of aviation.

Creativity: How will we show we understand in multiple ways?

- Role play – advising the farmer and understanding others' points of view.
- The art of curation – creating museum exhibits in interesting and creative ways.
- Making connections – between different modes of flight and how they operate.
- Creative writing and response – what does the world look like from the air?

Compassion

- Developing empathy with people from the past.
- Understanding multiple points of view.
- Understanding how the actions of some people can lead to consequences for others – the contribution the Wright brothers made to aviation and the impact of aviation on war. Also the impact of aviation on the environment – learning to understand that there are sometimes good and bad consequences of inventions.

Community

- An exhibition for the local community – inviting others into the History of Flight exhibition.
- Charitable action – raising money for air ambulances.
- Cultural capital:
  - » Learning about significant individuals in the past.
  - » Learning about the role of museums in communicating and curating information.
  - » Outdoor learning – designing their own flying machines and testing them out on the school grounds.

14

Overall outcome

- Information texts about our inherited culture and language. Exhibits and displays to be shared with visitors.

Narrative hook

- **People:** A thane and his villagers.
- **Place:** An Anglo-Saxon village near Hereford.
- **Problem:** Viking raids (in the 7th century Vikings attempted to make incursions into Hereford via the Wye and Severn rivers) and Celtic threats. How do we protect ourselves?
- **Possibilities:** Is it possible to negotiate with potential invaders? What can we learn from the past?

Year 4 (Autumn) – The Past

Can you judge a book by its cover? Challenging assumptions about ourselves and others.

Case study: Were the English ever really English (from AD 410 to 1066)?

Credibility: What will we learn?

- Who were the Angles, Saxons and Jutes and where did they come from?
- An understanding of the mix of cultures in Britain after the Romans left (including the Romans who stayed behind).
- The Vikings and their impact on British culture.
- Social structure (thanes, churls and thralls).
- The landscape of Britain in these times – forests (and wolves) and the growth of agricultural farmland. The importance of rivers for transport and trade.
- The impact of Anglo-Saxons on language.
- Anglo-Saxon stories, culture, beliefs, rituals and ways of life.
- Anglo-Saxons in our local area.
- The story of Beowulf and what it suggests about Anglo-Saxon values.

Coherence

- Connections to previous and future learning:
  - » Moving backwards in time from Year 3 and connecting to the Romans in Year 4 – the chronology of the curriculum.
  - » Connecting to the following unit on the Norman invasion of Britain.
- Connections to future units:
  - » Links to subsequent units connected to the theme of not judging a book by its cover – to indigenous people in South America in Unit 2 and to the concept of monsters in Unit 3.
- Connections to core learning:
  - » Maths – timelines. Time (using the sun to show the passage of time – sun dials). Area – mapping out the village.
  - » Literacy – see texts and written outcomes above. Drama and oracy embedded throughout.
  - » Reading for information and for creative interpretation.

Texts

Fiction: *Beowulf*, Celtic myths and legends, Viking myths.

Non-fiction: A variety of non-fiction texts about Anglo-Saxons and Vikings.

Written outcomes

Peace treaties, village records and historical accounts, letters, diaries, legends.

Link to curriculum intention

What does it mean to belong to a nation and how has our 'nationality' been shaped by invasion?

Key vocabulary

Anglo/Angleterre/English, assimilation, barrows, Celt, Christian, churl, culture, etymology, invasion, Norman, pagan, raid, Roman, runes, thane, thrall.

Our school values

Be determined – how determined did early Anglo-Saxons have to be to protect their land?

Be resilient – how did they cope with invasion?

Be peaceful (Second World War Week).

Creativity: How will we show we understand in multiple ways?

- Role play – building an Anglo-Saxon community.
- Designing an Anglo-Saxon village and working out how to protect it.
- Making connections – between migration, invasion and assimilation of cultures.
- Artistic life in Anglo-Saxon times – what instruments, arts and crafts did the Anglo-Saxons have and how might these have brought them comfort?

Compassion

- Developing empathy with people from the past.
- Understanding that England has always been made up of different cultures and 'tribes' and that its population is culturally mixed.
- Understanding multiple points of view.
- Understanding migration from the perspective of invasion and assimilation.
- Seeking peaceful solutions to problems – negotiating with the Vikings.

Community

- Opportunities for local experts and historians to come and talk to the children to link local and national history.
- Outdoor learning:
  » Midsummer Hillfort – why were hills important in defending yourself?
  » Offa's Dyke – what was it built from and why?
- Inviting the local community to come in and share our learning.

Bibliography

Allen-Kinross, P. (2019). Withdrawing Funding from the IB Will Be a 'Tragedy' for Social Mobility, Heads Warn, *Schools Week* (18 May). Available at: https://schoolsweek.co.uk/withdrawing-funding-from-the-ib-will-be-a-tragedy-for-social-mobility-heads-warn.

Arnold, M. (1993 [1875]). *Culture and Anarchy*, in *Culture and Anarchy and Other Writings*, ed. Stefan Collini (Cambridge: Cambridge University Press).

Ashman, G. (2017). Bad Times Ahead for Education in Wales, *Filling the Pail* (24 March) [blog]. Available at: https://gregashman.wordpress.com/2017/03/24/bad-times-ahead-for-education-in-wales.

BBC News (2019). Climate Strike: Thousands Protest Across UK (20 September). Available at: https://www.bbc.co.uk/news/uk-49767327.

Berger, R. (2003). *An Ethic of Excellence: Building a Culture of Craftsmanship with Students* (Portsmouth, NH: Heinemann).

Berger, R. (2014). *Leaders of Their Own Learning: Transforming Schools Through Student-Engaged Assessment* (San Francisco, CA: Jossey-Bass).

Bergland, C. (2013). The Neuroscience of Empathy, *Psychology Today* (10 October). Available at: https://www.psychologytoday.com/gb/blog/the-athletes-way/201310/the-neuroscience-empathy.

Blakemore, S.-J. (2018). *Inventing Ourselves: The Secret Life of the Teenage Brain* (New York: Doubleday).

British Academy and The Royal Society (2018). *The Impact of Artificial Intelligence on Work: An Evidence Synthesis on Implications for Individuals, Communities, and Societies*. Available at: https://www.thebritishacademy.ac.uk/sites/default/files/AI-and-work-evidence-synthesis.pdf.

Brown, P. C., Roediger III, H. L. and McDaniel, M. A. (2014). *Make It Stick: The Science of Successful Learning* (Cambridge, MA: Harvard University Press).

Cameron, D. (2016). Raising Attainment, Being Creative … and Surviving. Speech delivered at the University of Chichester Academy Trust conference, 5 September.

Christodoulou, D. (2013). *Seven Myths About Education* (Abingdon and New York: Routledge).

Counsell, C. (2018). Senior Curriculum Leadership 1: The Indirect Manifestation of Knowledge: (A) Curriculum As Narrative, *The Dignity of the Thing* (7 April) [blog]. Available at: https://thedignityofthethingblog.wordpress.com/2018/04/07/

senior-curriculum-leadership-1-the-indirect-manifestation-of-knowledge-a-curriculum-as-narrative.

Damasio, A. (2006). *Descartes' Error: Emotion, Reason and the Human Brain* (New York: Random House).

Dee, T. and Sievertsen, H. (2015). The Gift of Time: School Starting Age and Mental Health. NBER Working Paper No. 21610. Available at: https://www.nber.org/papers/w21610.

Department for Education (2013). *History Programmes of Study: Key Stages 1 and 2. National Curriculum in England* (September). DFE-00173-2013. Available at: https://assets.publishing.service.gov.uk/government/uploads/system/uploads/attachment_data/file/239035/PRIMARY_national_curriculum_-_History.pdf.

Department for Education (2019). *Timpson Review of School Exclusions* (May). Command Paper 92. Available at: https://assets.publishing.service.gov.uk/government/uploads/system/uploads/attachment_data/file/807862/Timpson_review.pdf.

Dickinson, E. (1951). ' "Hope" Is the Thing with Feathers', in *The Poems of Emily Dickinson*, ed. T. H. Johnson (Cambridge, MA: Belknap Press of Harvard University Press).

Donaldson, G. (2015). *Successful Futures: Independent Review of Curriculum and Assessment Arrangements in Wales* (February) (Cardiff: Welsh Government). Available at: https://gweddill.gov.wales/docs/dcells/publications/150225-successful-futures-en.pdf.

Duckworth, A. and Carlson, S. M. (2013). Self-Regulation and School Success, in B. W. Sokol, F. M. E. Grouzet, and U. Müller (eds), *Self-Regulation and Autonomy: Social and Developmental Dimensions of Human Conduct* (New York: Cambridge University Press), pp. 208–230. Available at: https://repository.upenn.edu/cgi/viewcontent.cgi?article=1002&context=psychology_papers.

Egan, K. (2008). *The Future of Education: Reimagining Our Schools from the Ground Up* (New Haven, CT: Yale University Press).

Fautley, M., Millard, E. and Hatcher, R. (2011). *Remaking the Curriculum: Re-engaging Young People in Secondary School* (Stoke-on-Trent: Trentham Books).

Forster, E. M. (2005 [1927]). *Aspects of the Novel* (London: Penguin).

Haberman, M. (1991). The Pedagogy of Poverty versus Good Teaching, *Kappan* 92(2): 81–87. Available at: https://www.pdkmembers.org/members_online/publications/Archive/pdf/PDK_92_2/81pdk_92_2.pdf.

Hargreaves, D. (2008). *Deep Learning – 2: Why Should They Learn?* (London: Specialist Schools and Academies Trust).

Hart, S., Dixon, A., Drummond, M. J. and McIntyre, D. (2004). *Learning without Limits* (Maidenhead: Open University Press).

Heathcote, D. and Bolton, G. (1995). *Drama for Learning: Dorothy Heathcote's Mantle of the Expert Approach to Education* (London: Heinemann).

Howard-Jones, P. (2018). *Evolution of the Learning Brain: Or How You Got to Be So Smart …* (Abingdon and New York: Routledge).

Humphrey, N., Curran, A., Morris, E., Farrell, P. and Woods, K. (2007). Emotional Intelligence and Education: A Critical Review, *Educational Psychology* 27(2): 235–254. Available at: https://www.researchgate.net/publication/233473746_Emotional_Intelligence_and_Education_A_critical_review.

Hyman, P. (2019). A Curriculum of Head, Heart and Hand, in R. Blatchford (ed.), *The Secondary Curriculum Leader's Handbook* (Woodbridge: John Catt Educational), pp. 13–27.

Illingworth, M. (2020). *Forget School: Why Young People Are Succeeding on Their Own Terms and What Schools Can Do to Avoid Being Left Behind* (Carmarthen: Independent Thinking Press).

International Baccalaureate (2016). Key Findings from Research on the Impact of the Diploma Programme. Available at: https://www.ibo.org/globalassets/publications/become-an-ib-school/research-dp-findings-en.pdf.

Kidd, D. (2005). Assessment As an Act of Love, *Teaching Times* 1.1: 33–37. Available at: https://library.teachingtimes.com/articles/assessment-as-an-act-of-love.

Kidd, D. (2013). Bouncing on a Bed of Knowledge (Or It's All About the Pedagogy, Stupid), *Love Learning* (8 May) [blog]. Available at: https://debra-kidd.com/2013/05/08/bouncing-on-a-bed-of-knowledge-or-its-all-about-the-pedagogy-stupid.

Kidd, D. (2015). *Becoming Mobius: The Complex Matter of Education* (Carmarthen: Independent Thinking Press).

Kim, M. C. and Hannafin, M. J. (2011). Scaffolding 6th Graders' Problem-Solving in Technology-Enhanced Science Classrooms: A Qualitative Case Study, *Instructional Science: An International Journal of the Learning Sciences* 39(3): 255–282.

Kirschner, P. A., Sweller, J., Kirschner, F. and Zambrano, J. (2018). From Cognitive Load Theory to Collaborative Cognitive Load Theory, *International Journal of Computer-Supported Collaborative Learning* 13(2): 213–233. Available at: https://doi.org/10.1007/s11412-018-9277-y.

Kuepper-Tetzel, C. (2017). Embedded Phenomena: Increasing Comprehension of STEM Concepts Using Body and Space, *The Learning Scientists* (21 September) [blog]. Available at: http://www.learningscientists.org/blog/2017/9/21-1.

Lear, J. (2019). Conference Keynote. Speech delivered at the Bringing the Curriculum to Life conference, Blackburn, 29 November.

Lui, C., Solis, S. L., Jensen, H., Hopkins, E., Neale, D., Zosh, J., Hirsh-Pasek, K. and Whitebread, D. (2017). *Neuroscience and Learning Through Play: A Review of the Evidence* (Billund: LEGO Foundation). Available at: https://www.legofoundation.com/media/1064/neuroscience-review_web.pdf.

Lyster, R. and Saito, K. (2010). Oral Feedback in Classroom SLA: A Meta-Analysis, *Studies in Second Language Acquisition* 32(2): 265–302.

Magnuson, C. D. and Barnett, L. A. (2013). The Playful Advantage: How Playfulness Enhances Coping with Stress, *Leisure Sciences* 35(2): 129–144.

Michaels, S., O'Connor, C. and Resnick, L. B. (2008). Deliberative Discourse Idealized and Realized: Accountable Talk in the Classroom and in Civic Life, *Studies in Philosophy and Education* 27(4): 283–297.

Mweti, R. (2018). We Are Scientists, *Hatching Minds* (25 August) [blog]. Available at: https://migratingbirdteaching.com/2018/08/25/we-are-scientists.

Myatt, M. (2016). *High Challenge, Low Threat: How the Best Leaders Find the Balance* (Woodbridge: John Catt Educational).

Myatt, M. (2018). *The Curriculum: Gallimaufry to Coherence* (Woodbridge: John Catt Educational).

Newmark, B. (2019). Why Teach?, *BENNEWMARK* (10 February) [blog]. Available at: https://bennewmark.wordpress.com/2019/02/10/why-teach.

Noë, A. (2009). *Out of Our Heads: Why You Are Not Your Brain, and Other Lessons from the Biology of Consciousness* (New York: Hill & Wang).

Offer, A. (2006). *The Challenge of Affluence: Self-Control and Well-Being in the United States and Britain since 1950* (New York: Oxford University Press).

Ofsted (2015). *Key Stage 3: The Wasted Years?* (September). Ref: 150106. Available at: https://www.gov.uk/government/publications/key-stage-3-the-wasted-years.

Ofsted (2017). *Bold Beginnings: The Reception Curriculum in a Sample of Good and Outstanding Primary Schools* (November). Ref: 170045. Available at: https://assets.publishing.service. gov.uk/government/uploads/system/uploads/attachment_data/file/663560/28933_ Ofsted_-_Early_Years_Curriculum_Report_-_Accessible.pdf.

Ofsted (2018). *An Investigation into How to Assess the Quality of Education Through Curriculum Intent, Implementation and Impact* (December). Ref: 180035. Available at: https://www.gov. uk/government/publications/curriculum-research-assessing-intent-implementation-and-impact.

Ofsted (2019a). *The Education Inspection Framework* (January). Ref: 180039. Available at: https://assets.publishing.service.gov.uk/government/uploads/system/uploads/ attachment_data/file/801581/Proposed_Education_Inspection_Framework_draft_for_ consultation_140119_archived.pdf.

Ofsted (2019b). *The Education Inspection Framework* (May). Ref: 190015. Available at: https://www.gov.uk/government/publications/education-inspection-framework.

Ofsted and Spielman, A. (2017). HMCI's Commentary: Recent Primary and Secondary Curriculum Research (11 October). Available at: https://www.gov.uk/government/ speeches/hmcis-commentary-october-2017.

Ofsted and Spielman, A. (2018). HMCI Commentary: Curriculum and the New Education Inspection Framework (18 September). Available at: https://www.gov.uk/government/speeches/hmci-commentary-curriculum-and-the-new-education-inspection-framework.

Paas, F. and Sweller, J. (2012). An Evolutionary Upgrade of Cognitive Load Theory: Using the Human Motor System and Collaboration to Support the Learning of Complex Cognitive Tasks, *Educational Psychology Review* 24(1): 27–45. Available at: https://link.springer.com/article/10.1007/s10648-011-9179-2.

Palmer, L. L. and DeBoer, B. (2014). Enhancing Early Reading Recognition and Phonemic Awareness with Neuro-Educational Programming: The Minnesota SMART Project (Stimulating Maturity through Accelerated Readiness Training). An Interim Report (May). Available at: https://actg.org/sites/actg.org/files/documents/MinnesotaSMARTProject_May2004.pdf.

Pearce, C. (2010). The Life of Suggestions, *Qualitative Inquiry* 17(7): 902–908.

Puntambekar, S. and Kolodner, J. L. (2005). Toward Implementing Distributed Scaffolding: Helping Students Learn Science from Design, *Journal of Research in Science Teaching* 42(2): 185–217.

Roberts, H. (2012). *Oops! Helping Children Learn Accidentally* (Carmarthen: Independent Thinking Press).

Roberts, H. and Kidd, D. (2018). *Uncharted Territories: Adventures in Learning* (Carmarthen: Independent Thinking Press).

Roediger III, H. L., Putnam, A. L. and Smith, M. A. (2011). Ten Benefits of Testing and Their Applications to Educational Practice, *Reading Research Quarterly* 21(1): 49–58.

Rundell, K. (2017). *The Explorer* (London: Bloomsbury Children's Books).

Sealy, C. (2017). The 3D Curriculum That Promotes Remembering, *Primarytimerydotcom* (28 October) [blog]. Available at: https://primarytimery.com/2017/10/28/the-3d-curriculum-that-promotes-remembering.

Seligman, M. E. P. (2002). *Authentic Happiness: Using the New Positive Psychology to Realize Your Potential for Lasting Fulfillment* (New York: Free Press).

Singh, A., Uijtdewilligen, L., Twisk, J. W. R., van Mechelen, W. and Chinapaw, M. J. M. (2012). Physical Activity and Performance at School: A Systematic Review of the Literature Including a Methodological Quality Assessment, *Archives of Pediatrics and Adolescent Medicine* 166(1): 49–55. Available at: https://jamanetwork.com/journals/jamapediatrics/fullarticle/1107683.

Smith, M. (2017). *The Emotional Learner: Understanding Emotions, Learners and Achievement* (Abingdon and New York: Routledge).

Staufenberg, J. (2019). Half of Schools Start GCSEs in Year 9, NFER Survey Suggests, *Schools Week* (12 April). Available at: https://schoolsweek.co.uk/half-of-schools-start-gcses-in-year-9-nfer-survey-suggests.

Sweller, J. (1988). Cognitive Load During Problem Solving: Effects on Learning, *Cognitive Science* 12(2): 257–285.

Tan, S. (2007). *The Arrival* (London: Hodder Children's Books).

Taylor, T. (2017). *A Beginner's Guide to Mantle of the Expert: A Transformative Approach to Education* (Norwich: Singular Publishing).

Wade, S. and Kidd, C. (2019). The Role of Prior Knowledge and Curiosity in Learning, *Psychonomic Bulletin and Review* 26(4): 1377–1387.

Waters, M. (2013). *Thinking Allowed: On Schooling* (Carmarthen: Independent Thinking Press).

Watson, S. (2019). Aim High, Work Smart, Care Deeply, in R. Blatchford (ed.), *The Secondary Curriculum Leader's Handbook* (Woodbridge: John Catt Educational), pp. 53–60.

Weale, S. (2019). More Than 49,000 Pupils 'Disappeared' from English Schools – Study, *The Guardian* (18 April). Available at: https://www.theguardian.com/education/2019/apr/18/more-than-49000-pupils-disappeared-from-schools-study.

White, R. E., Prager, E. O., Schaefer, C., Kross, E., Duckworth, A. L. and Carlson, S. M. (2017). The 'Batman Effect': Improving Perseverance in Young Children, *Child Development* 88(5): 1563–1571.

Whitebread, D., Basilio, M., Kuvalja, M. and Verma, M. (2012). *The Importance of Play: A Report on the Value of Children's Play with a Series of Policy Recommendations* (Brussels: Toy Industries of Europe). Available at: http://www.importanceofplay.eu/IMG/pdf/dr_david_whitebread_-_the_importance_of_play.pdf.

Wiliam, D. (2013). *Redesigning Schooling – 3: Principled Curriculum Design* (London: Specialist Schools and Academies Trust). Available at https://webcontent.ssatuk.co.uk/wp-content/uploads/2013/09/Dylan-Wiliam-Principled-curriculum-design-chapter-1.pdf.

Willingham, D. T. (2004). Ask the Cognitive Scientist: The Privileged Status of Story, *American Educator* (summer). Available at: http://www.aft.org/periodical/american-educator/summer-2004/ask-cognitive-scientist.

Willingham, D. T. (2009). Why Don't Students Like School? Because the Mind Is Not Designed for Thinking, *American Educator* (spring). Available at: https://www.aft.org/sites/default/files/periodicals/WILLINGHAM%282%29.pdf.

Zimmer, H. D. and Cohen, R. L. (2001). Remembering Actions: A Specific Type of Memory?, in H. D. Zimmer, R. L. Cohen, M. J. Guynn, J. Engelkamp, R. Kormi-Nouri and M. A. Foley (eds), *Memory for Action: A Distinct Form of Episodic Memory* (New York: Oxford University Press), pp. 3–24.

Teaching: Notes From The Front Line
We are, at the time I write this, in need of a revolution in education. This is a strong statement and I don't use it lightly
Dr Debra Kidd
ISBN: 978-178135131-4

Our current education system is overloaded with amendments, additions and adjustments which have been designed to keep an outdated model in the air. But it is crashing. And as it comes down, we see the battle of blame begin. It is time to take our vocation back, to learn to trust ourselves and each other and, crucially, to take control of the direction of education and policy.

This is a narrative of hope, of how the system could be different. It offers tales from within the classroom of learning, of hope, of laughter, of gentle subversion. This is a call to arms for a pedagogical revolution. Will you answer it?

Becoming Mobius
The complex matter of education
Dr Debra Kidd
ISBN: 978-178135219-9

Drawing predominantly on the philosophy of Gilles Deleuze, *Becoming Mobius* argues that teachers can and should learn to love uncertainty and complexity; that they should seek to become pedagogical activists working within a system while remaining outside of it – becoming like a Mobius strip both in and out. It argues that the interesting stuff in classrooms exists in the minute details, the pivotal moments of interactions, in relationships and in the affective dimension, and that having faith in becoming attuned – and listening to the 'gutterances' of others – leads teaching into a new world of possibility.

This is an honest, challenging and incredibly profound book that makes you stop and think – deeply – about what you do, why you do it and the effect it has. You will never look at teaching in the same light again.

Uncharted Territories

Adventures in learning

Hywel Roberts and Debra Kidd

ISBN: 978-178135295-3

Rooted in practice and grounded in research, *Uncharted Territories* invites a reassessment of what curriculum coverage can look like and provides an abundance of hooks into exploratory learning that place learners – of whatever age – knee-deep in dilemma, so that they are thinking deeply, analytically and imaginatively. These are not knowledge organisers or schemes of work; rather they are inspirational forays into imagined contexts for learning which, as fantastical as they may appear, always have the real world as their destination. Signposted by story starters and inductive questions – not to mention the beautiful illustrations which are sure to fire children's imaginations – Hywel and Debra's innovative routes to learning will help teachers stray from the beaten track of the curriculum and instil in learners a sense of purpose as they discover, manipulate and apply knowledge and skills across a range of collaborative, cross-curricular problem-solving contexts.

While *Uncharted Territories* is a rallying call to arms for the imagination, in each of its chapters Hywel and Debra also delve into the why in order to present the teacher with a comprehensive debrief of the learning processes and the theoretical and academic underpinning. Furthermore, the authors provide a helpful listing of drama techniques and relevant books and poems that can be incorporated into the learning journeys, as well as useful advice on how to assess and evidence their outcomes.

Designed for use with learners of all ages, from early years to secondary.